GALATIANS:
No other Gospel

ROBERT GRIFFITH

Copyright © 2025 Grace and Truth Publishing

All rights reserved. No part of this book may be reproduced, stored in a retrieval system, or transmitted in any form, without the written permission of Grace and Truth Publishing.

GRACE AND TRUTH PUBLISHING
PO Box 338, Gunnedah NSW 2380 Australia
www.graceandtruthpublishing.com.au

All Bible quotes are from the New International Version (NIV) expect where otherwise stated.

NEW INTERNATIONAL VERSION (NIV), Copyright 1973, 1978 and 1984 by international Bible Society. Used by permission of Zondervan Publishing House. All rights reserved.

Other version quotes are from:

AMPLIFIED BIBLE (AMP), Copyright © 1954, 1958, 1962, 1964, 1965, 1987 by The Lockman Foundation. Used by permission.

ENGLISH STANDARD VERSION (ESV), Copyright © 2001 by Crossway Bibles, a division of Good News Publishers. Used by permission. All rights reserved.

NEW AMERICAN STANDARD BIBLE (NASB), Copyright © 1960, 1962, 1963, 1968, 1971, 1972, 1973, 1975, 1977, by The Lockman Foundation. Used by permission.

NEW KING JAMES VERSION (NKJV), Copyright © 1979, 1980, 1982, by Thomas Nelson Inc. Used by permission. All rights reserved.

THE MESSAGE (MSG), by Eugene Peterson, Copyright © 1993, 1994, 1995, 1996, and 2000. Used by permission of NavPress Publishing Group. All rights reserved.

REVISED STANDARD VERSION (RSV), Copyright © 1973, by Thomas Nelson Inc. Used by permission. All rights reserved.

Quotes in square brackets are the author's comment.

ISBN 978-1-7635504-1-4

TABLE OF CONTENTS

1. Desertion and Deception 5

2. Paul's Divine Commission 17

3. Unity in the Gospel 27

4. Standing Firm 39

5. Faith not Works 52

6. The Promise and the Law 63

7. No Longer Slaves 74

8. Paul's Heartfelt Plea 85

9. Freedom in Christ 98

10. Standing Firm in Freedom 111

11. Walking in the Spirit 125

12. Living in Christ 136

1. DESERTION AND DECEPTION

As we embark upon this journey through Paul's letter to the Galatians, it is crucial to understand the context, purpose, and significance of this very powerful epistle. The book of Galatians stands as a beacon of truth and freedom in the New Testament, addressing the core issues of faith, grace, and the law.

The Apostle Paul wrote this letter to the churches in Galatia, a region in modern-day Turkey. Unlike his other epistles, which were often addressed to specific congregations, the Galatians letter was intended for a group of churches within a particular region. This indicates that the various issues Paul addressed were widespread and pressing among the believers there.

The Galatian churches were composed of both Jewish and Gentile converts. This diversity became a breeding ground for conflict, especially concerning the role of the Mosaic Law in the life of a Christian. False teachers, often referred to as Judaizers, had infiltrated the churches, teaching that Gentile converts must now also adhere to Jewish customs, particularly circumcision, to be truly saved.

Purpose of the Letter

Paul's primary purpose in writing to the Galatians was to defend the gospel of grace and to reaffirm the believers' freedom in Christ. He passionately argued that salvation is by grace alone, through faith in Jesus Christ and not by works of the law. This message was crucial because the very essence of the gospel was under threat. Paul expresses his astonishment at how quickly the Galatians were turning to a different gospel:

Galatians 1:6-7 *"I am astonished that you are so quickly deserting the one who called you to live in the grace of Christ and are turning to a different gospel - which is really no gospel at all. Evidently some people are throwing you into confusion and are trying to pervert the gospel of Christ."*

Four Key Themes

1. Justification by grace through faith: One of the central themes of Galatians is that justification - being declared righteous before God – comes by grace and is embraced by faith in Jesus Christ, not by observing the law. Paul succinctly states this in chapter 2:

> **Galatians 2:16** *"... know that a person is not justified by the works of the law, but by faith in Jesus Christ. So we, too, have put our faith in Christ Jesus that we may be justified by faith in Christ and not by the works of the law, because by the works of the law no one will be justified."*

2. Christian freedom: Paul emphasizes the freedom believers have in Christ. This freedom is not a license to sin but a liberation from the bondage of the law and sin.

> **Galatians 5:1** *"It is for freedom that Christ has set us free. Stand firm, then, and do not let yourselves be burdened again by a yoke of slavery."*

3. The role of the Law: While the law serves a purpose, it is not the path to salvation. Paul explains the law's role as a tutor and guardian leading us to Christ, Who fulfills all the requirements of the law.

> **Galatians 3:24** *"So the law was our guardian until Christ came that we might be justified by faith."*

4. Life in the Spirit: Paul contrasts living by the flesh with living by the Spirit. He exhorts believers to walk by the Spirit, producing the fruit of the Spirit in their lives.

Galatians 5:22-23 *"But the fruit of the Spirit is love, joy, peace, forbearance, kindness, goodness, faithfulness, gentleness and self-control. Against such things there is no law."*

Significance for Today

The book of Galatians is as relevant today as it was when it was written. In a world where legalism and the pressure to conform to religious requirements continues to infiltrate the church, Paul's message of grace and freedom remains vital. It challenges us to examine the foundations of our faith, to live in the freedom Christ provides, and to rely wholly upon His grace, His empowering presence.

As we delve into this epistle, I encourage you to open your heart to its truths, allowing the Holy Spirit to transform your understanding and deepen your relationship with Jesus Christ. My prayer is that this study of Galatians will renew your appreciation for the gospel and fortify your resolve to stand firm in the freedom that the life, death and resurrection of Jesus Christ has secured for you.

In this opening chapter I want us to work through the first ten verses of chapter one. In this letter, Paul passionately defends the true gospel against any distortion, reminding us that salvation comes through grace alone, by faith alone, in Christ alone.

As we examine these opening verses, we will explore Paul's apostolic authority, his astonishment at the Galatians' desertion, and the dire consequences of preaching a false gospel.

Galatians 1:1-10 *"Paul, an apostle - sent not from men nor by a man, but by Jesus Christ and God the Father, who raised him from the dead - and all the brothers and sisters with me, to the churches in Galatia: Grace and peace to you from God our Father and the Lord Jesus Christ, who gave himself for our sins to rescue us from the present evil age, according to the will of our God and Father, to whom be glory for ever and ever. Amen.*

I am astonished that you are so quickly deserting the one who called you to live in the grace of Christ and are turning to a different gospel - which is really no gospel at all. Evidently some people are throwing you into confusion and are trying to pervert the gospel of Christ. But even if we or an angel from heaven should preach a gospel other than the one we preached to you, let them be under God's curse!

As we have already said, so now I say again: If anybody is preaching to you a gospel other than what you accepted, let them be under God's curse! Am I now trying to win the approval of human beings, or of God? Or am I trying to please people? If I were still trying to please people, I would not be a servant of Christ."

Paul's Apostolic Authority (Verses 1-2)

Paul opens his letter by asserting his apostolic authority, stating unequivocally that his commission came not from men, but from Jesus Christ and God the Father.

This declaration is critical, as it establishes the divine authority behind his message. In a world which was full of false teachers, Paul knew how important it was to show his readers that he was called by God and was speaking the Truth.

Paul's identity and authority ...

Paul identifies himself as an apostle. The term 'apostle' means 'one who is sent.' However, Paul clarifies that his apostleship is not of human origin. He wasn't appointed by any human council or through human lineage but was directly commissioned by Jesus Christ and God the Father.

This divine appointment sets Paul apart and underscores the authority and authenticity of his message. In Acts 9, we read about Paul's dramatic conversion on the road to Damascus, where Jesus Himself called Paul to be an apostle to the Gentiles. This calling was unique and powerful, shaping Paul's whole ministry and message.

In today's world, the whole concept of authority is often questioned or challenged. Many of us have experienced situations where certain authority figures have failed or disappointed us. But Paul's authority is not derived from human institutions, which are fallible, but from his infallible God. This distinction is crucial for us understanding the weight and reliability of Paul's message to the Galatians.

The source of Paul's authority ...

Paul emphasizes that his authority comes from *"Jesus Christ and God the Father, who raised him from the dead."* This resurrection power not only validated Jesus as the Son of God but it also authenticated Paul's apostleship. The resurrection is the cornerstone of the whole Christian faith, affirming that Jesus Christ has conquered sin and death. Therefore, Paul's gospel, rooted in the resurrection, carries the full weight and authority of God. The resurrection is not merely a past event; it is a present reality with ongoing implications. It is the power that transforms lives, bringing hope and assurance of eternal life.

When Paul speaks of the resurrection, he speaks of the very foundation of the Christian faith. This resurrection power also implies that any gospel contrary to the one rooted in the resurrection is fundamentally flawed.

The fellowship of believers ...

Paul extends his greeting with *"all the brothers and sisters with me."* This inclusion signifies the unity and collective witness of the Christian community. It wasn't just Paul standing alone; he was supported by a community of believers who affirmed the same gospel. This communal aspect is essential, as it reflects the shared faith and mission of the early church.

In our individualistic culture today, we often overlook the importance of community. The early church thrived on communal faith, support, and accountability. Paul's mention of "*all the brothers and sisters*" with him serves as a reminder that the gospel is not just a personal faith; it is a faith lived in community. We are part of a larger body of believers, and our faith is always strengthened when we are together.

The Gospel of Grace and Peace (Verses 3-5)

After establishing his authority, Paul extends a blessing of grace and peace from God the Father and the Lord Jesus Christ. This greeting, common in most of Paul's letters, is more than a formality – it encapsulates the essence of the gospel.

Grace and peace ...

The terms *grace* and *peace* are very rich with theological significance. Grace (Greek: *'charis'*) refers to God's amazing grace towards His children, the free gift of salvation offered to sinners.

Peace (Greek: *eirēnē*) denotes the restored relationship between God and humanity through Christ. Together, they summarize the gospel: through grace, we receive peace with God.

Grace is the foundation of our faith. It is the empowering presence of God, poured out upon us in Christ. We cannot earn it; we can only receive it. This concept is certainly countercultural. In a world today that values personal achievement, grace stands as a radical notion that God's love and favour is given so freely to whom He chooses.

This grace leads to peace, a peace that transcends all understanding, a peace that guards our hearts and minds in Christ Jesus (Philippians 4:7).

Christ's sacrifice and deliverance ...

Paul reminds the Galatians that Jesus *"gave himself for our sins to rescue us from the present evil age."* This statement highlights two critical aspects of the gospel: substitution and deliverance. Jesus' sacrifice was substitutionary - He actually took our place, bearing the penalty for our sins. Furthermore, His death and resurrection deliver us from the power and influence of this evil age. The term *"rescue"* implies a dire situation from which we can never save ourselves; only the intervention of Jesus can deliver us.

"The present evil age" refers to the current world system that is in opposition to God's kingdom. It is marked by sin, corruption, and rebellion against God. The sacrifice of Jesus rescues us from this age, not by removing us from it, but by transforming us within it. As believers, we are *in* the world but not *of* the world. We are called to live distinctively, reflecting the values of the kingdom of Heaven in the midst of the broken, dysfunctional kingdom of this world.

The will of God the Father …

This rescue operation is *"according to the will of our God and Father."* The gospel is deeply rooted in the sovereign will and eternal plan of God. It was God's will to send His Son to redeem humanity, demonstrating His love, mercy, and grace. This divine initiative underscores that salvation is entirely God's work, from start to finish.

The will of God is central to understanding our salvation. It reminds us that our salvation is not an afterthought or a contingency plan. It is the unfolding of God's eternal purpose. God's will is good, pleasing, and perfect (Romans 12:2). Understanding that our salvation is part of God's sovereign will give us assurance and security. It means that our salvation is not dependent upon our own fluctuating faithfulness but on God's unchanging purpose.

Glory to God forever …

Paul concludes this opening greeting with a doxology: *"to whom be glory for ever and ever. Amen."* This spontaneous outburst of praise reflects Paul's deep gratitude and reverence for God's redemptive work. It serves as a reminder that all glory and honour belong to God alone, not to any human effort or achievement.

Doxology, or praise, is always the proper response to understanding the gospel. When we grasp the magnitude of God's grace and the depth of His love, our hearts overflow with praise. Giving glory to God is not a religious formality; it is the natural response of a heart transformed by the gospel. It shifts our focus from ourselves to God, acknowledging His sovereignty, His goodness, and His majesty.

Paul's Astonishment and Rebuke (Verses 6-9)

Paul transitions from his greeting to an expression of astonishment and rebuke. He is shocked that the Galatians are turning away from the true gospel to embrace a distorted version.

Desertion and deception ...

Paul is "*astonished*" that the Galatians are "*so quickly deserting the one who called you to live in the grace of Christ.*" The term 'deserting' (Greek: *metatithesthe*) conveys the idea of a military rebellion or a shift in allegiance. The Galatians are abandoning the grace of Christ, which they had initially embraced, to follow a different gospel. This swift desertion is perplexing and deeply troubling to Paul.

Desertion from the gospel is not just a doctrinal error; it is a relational betrayal. It is turning away from the One Who called us into grace. Paul's astonishment reflects his deep concern for the Galatians' spiritual well-being. The speed at which they are turning away suggests that they were not deeply rooted in the true gospel. This should prompt us to examine our own commitment to the gospel. Are we firmly rooted in grace, or are we susceptible to turning away when faced with false teaching?

A different gospel ...

Paul clarifies that this "*different gospel*" is no gospel at all. The term *gospel* (Greek: *euangelion*) means "*good news.*" Any deviation from the true gospel is, by definition, not good news but a perversion. The false teachers, often referred to as Judaizers, were advocating a gospel that required adherence to the Jewish law in addition to faith in Christ.

This distortion undermined the sufficiency of Christ's sacrifice and introduced legalism into the equation of salvation.

Legalism, the attempt to earn God's favour through adherence to laws and regulations, is a perversion of the true gospel of God's grace. It adds human effort to divine accomplishment, suggesting that Christ's sacrifice is not sufficient. Paul's vehement opposition to legalism is a reminder that the true gospel is based solely on God's grace. Any addition to the gospel is a subtraction from the gospel's power and truth.

The source of confusion ...

Paul notes that *"some people are throwing you into confusion and are trying to pervert the gospel of Christ."* These false teachers were creating chaos and leading the Galatians astray. Their teaching was not just different interpretations but an outright perversion of the true gospel. Paul's strong language indicates the seriousness of the issue – any alteration of the gospel message is a grave offense.

Confusion in the church often arises from distorted teachings. It creates division and uncertainty, leading believers away from the simplicity and purity of devotion to Christ. Paul's concern for the Galatians highlights the need for discernment in the church. We must be vigilant in guarding the truth of the gospel and addressing false teachings that lead to confusion and division.

Anathema: The consequence of false teaching ...

Paul issues a severe warning: *"But even if we or an angel from heaven should preach a gospel other than the one we preached to you, let them be under God's curse!"*

The term "*curse*" (Greek: *anathema*) signifies being cut off from Christ and condemned. Paul repeats this warning in verse 9 for emphasis. The repetition underscores the gravity of preaching a false gospel. Paul's dramatic language also conveys the seriousness with which we must guard the purity of the gospel.

The term *anathema* is strong and unambiguous. It conveys the idea of being set apart for destruction. Paul's use of this term highlights the eternal consequences of distorting the gospel. False teaching is not a minor issue; it has eternal ramifications. This sobering reality should drive us to always uphold the truth of the gospel with unwavering commitment.

Seeking God's Approval (Verse 10)

Paul concludes this section by addressing his motivations and integrity as a servant of Christ. He rhetorically asks, *"Am I now trying to win the approval of human beings, or of God? Or am I trying to please people?"* His critics may have accused him of seeking human approval by preaching a message of grace rather than legalistic adherence to the law.

However, Paul clarifies that his primary aim is always to please God, not humans. His unwavering commitment to the true gospel, despite opposition, attests to his integrity and dedication. The temptation to please people rather than God is a constant challenge. In ministry and in our personal lives, the desire for human approval can subtly influence our actions and decisions.

Paul's statement here challenges us to examine our own motivations. Are we seeking to please people or God? True discipleship involves a commitment to please God, even when it means facing opposition or criticism.

The cost of discipleship ...

Paul declares, *"If I were still trying to please people, I would not be a servant of Christ."* True discipleship often involves standing against popular opinion and facing persecution. Paul's allegiance to Christ supersedes any desire for human approval. This principle challenges us to examine our own motivations - are we more concerned with pleasing people or remaining faithful to Christ?

Being a servant of Christ is costly. It requires a willingness to stand firm in the truth, even when it is unpopular. Paul's example teaches us that faithfulness to Christ is paramount, and it often comes with a price. But the reward is far greater - eternal life and the approval of our Lord and Savior.

Conclusion

As we reflect on Galatians 1:1-10, we are reminded of the centrality and the purity of the gospel. Paul's passionate defense underscores that any deviation from the gospel of grace is a serious offense with eternal consequences. The gospel is the good news of Jesus Christ, Who gave Himself for our sins to rescue us from this present evil age. It is a message rooted in the sovereign will of God, accomplished through the power of the resurrection, and designed to bring glory to God alone.

In a world filled with competing voices and false teaching, we must remain steadfast in the truth of the gospel. Like Paul, let us boldly proclaim the grace and peace that come through Jesus Christ, resisting any attempt to distort or dilute this glorious message. May we seek to please God above all, living as faithful servants of Christ, to the glory of God forever.

2. PAUL'S DIVINE COMMISSION

As we continue our journey through the book of Galatians, we will be focusing now on verses Galatians 1:11-24 where Paul shares his testimony, underscoring the divine origin of his gospel and the transformative power of God's grace in his life. His story is a powerful reminder that the gospel is not man-made but divinely revealed.

> **Galatians 1:11-24** *"I want you to know, brothers and sisters, that the gospel I preached is not of human origin. I did not receive it from any man, nor was I taught it; rather, I received it by revelation from Jesus Christ. For you have heard of my previous way of life in Judaism, how intensely I persecuted the church of God and tried to destroy it. I was advancing in Judaism beyond many of my own age among my people and was extremely zealous for the traditions of my fathers.*
>
> *But when God, who set me apart from my mother's womb and called me by his grace, was pleased to reveal his Son in me so that I might preach him among the Gentiles, my immediate response was not to consult any human being. I did not go up to Jerusalem to see those who were apostles before I was, but I went into Arabia. Later I returned to Damascus.*
>
> *Then after three years, I went up to Jerusalem to get acquainted with Cephas and stayed with him fifteen days. I saw none of the other apostles - only James, the Lord's brother. I assure you before God that what I am writing you is no lie. Then I went to Syria and Cilicia. I was personally unknown to the churches of Judea that are in Christ. They only heard the report: "The man who formerly persecuted us is now preaching the faith he once tried to destroy." And they praised God because of me.*

The Divine Origin of Paul's Gospel (Verses 11-12)

Paul begins this section by asserting that the gospel he is preaching is not from human origin. This claim is crucial because it establishes the divine authority and authenticity of his message.

Revelation, not tradition ...

Paul emphasizes that he did not receive the gospel from any human being, nor was he taught it by any man. Instead, he received it by revelation from Jesus Christ. This revelation came via a direct and personal encounter with the risen Christ, which transformed Paul from a persecutor of the church into its most passionate advocate.

In Acts chapter 9, we read about Paul's dramatic conversion on the road to Damascus, where Jesus Himself appeared to Paul and commissioned him as an Apostle to the Gentiles. This direct revelation sets Paul apart and reinforces the divine origin of his message.

The authority of revelation ...

The concept of revelation is fundamental to understanding the authority of the gospel Paul preached. Revelation implies that the message comes directly from God, without human mediation.

This divine origin gives the gospel its ultimate authority and guarantees its purity. Unlike human traditions or teachings, which can be flawed or corrupted, divine revelation is perfect and unchanging.

Paul's insistence on the revelatory nature of his gospel serves to reassure the Galatians that the Apostle's message is trustworthy and authoritative.

The uniqueness of Paul's calling ...

Paul's calling was unique in that it involved a direct encounter with Christ. This encounter not only changed the course of his life but also confirmed his Apostolic authority.

Paul's testimony serves as a powerful reminder that God can use anyone, regardless of their past, to accomplish His purposes. It also underlines the transformative power of the gospel, which can turn even the fiercest opponent into a devoted follower.

Paul's Past Life and Transformation (Verses 13-14)

Paul continues by recounting his past life in Judaism and his radical transformation through God's amazing grace.

Paul's zeal in Judaism ...

Paul describes his former way of life in Judaism, emphasizing how intensely he persecuted the church and tried to destroy it. He was advancing in Judaism beyond many of his peers and was extremely zealous for the traditions of his fathers.

Paul's passion and reputation in Judaism highlight his deep commitment to his religious beliefs and his active role in opposing the early Christian movement.

Paul's background as a zealous Jew and a persecutor of the church is significant because it reinforces the dramatic nature of his conversion. He was not a passive observer but an active opponent of Christianity.

His transformation, therefore, is a powerful testimony to the grace of God and the truth of the gospel.

Persecution of the Church ...

Paul's persecution of the church was intense and relentless. In Acts 8:3, we read that Paul began to destroy the church, going from house to house, dragging off both men and women and putting them in prison. Paul's actions were driven by his zeal for the Jewish law and his genuine belief that the Christian movement was a threat to the purity of Judaism. His persecution was not just a simple intellectual disagreement but rather a violent and determined attempt to completely eradicate the followers of Christ.

Advancement in Judaism ...

Paul's rapid advancement in Judaism and his zeal for the traditions of his fathers, indicate that he was highly regarded within the Jewish community. He was a rising star, likely destined for a prominent position within the religious establishment. This background adds weight to his testimony, as it shows that he had so much to lose by converting to Christianity. His willingness to abandon his prestigious position and embrace the gospel, demonstrates the profound impact of his encounter with Christ.

God's Sovereign Call and Revelation (Verses 15-16)

Paul then highlights the divine initiative in his calling and the revelation of Jesus Christ.

God's sovereign choice ...

Paul states that God *"set me apart from my mother's womb and called me by his grace."* This language echoes the Old Testament calling of prophets like Jeremiah (Jeremiah 1:5) and Isaiah (Isaiah 49:1). Paul's use of this language emphasizes that his apostleship was not a matter of personal ambition but a divine calling.

God had a specific purpose for Paul's life, and He orchestrated events to bring Paul to the point of conversion and commission. The idea of being set apart from birth highlights the sovereignty of God in salvation and ministry.

It also reminds us that God has a plan and purpose for each of our lives, even before we are born. Our calling and destiny are not accidents of history but part of God's eternal design. This truth provides assurance and confidence as we seek to follow God's will for our lives.

Revelation of Christ ...

Paul explains that God was pleased *"to reveal his Son in me so that I might preach him among the Gentiles."* The revelation of Christ was not merely an external vision but an internal transformation.

Paul's encounter with Christ on the road to Damascus was a turning point that radically changed his identity, his mission, his message and his whole life. This revelation was not for Paul's benefit alone but for the purpose of preaching Christ among the Gentiles.

The phrase *"reveal his Son in me"* suggests a deep, personal, and transformative experience of Christ. It speaks to the intimate and powerful nature of Paul's conversion. This internal revelation equipped Paul for his mission to the Gentiles, demonstrating that true ministry flows from a personal encounter with Jesus Christ.

Immediate obedience ...

Paul's immediate response to this revelation was not to consult any human being or seek validation from the apostles in Jerusalem. Instead, he went into Arabia and later returned to Damascus.

This period of retreat and reflection highlights Paul's reliance on God's guidance rather than human approval. It also emphasizes his immediate obedience to God's call, without hesitation or delay.

Paul's journey into Arabia and subsequent return to Damascus indicate a period of solitude and preparation. This time alone with God allowed Paul to deepen his understanding of the gospel and prepare him for his future ministry. It serves as a reminder that sometimes, God calls us to step away from the busyness of life and spend time in His presence, seeking His guidance and preparing for the work He has planned for us.

Application

These verses provide significant insights into Paul's understanding of his role and the nature of the gospel. Several key applications can be drawn. Just as Paul was set apart for a specific purpose, every believer is called by God for a unique role in His kingdom.

Understanding and embracing this calling is crucial for effective ministry. Paul's calling (and ours too) was grace centered - not based on our own merits but on God's grace. This fosters humility and dependence on God.

The personal and transformative nature of encountering Christ is essential for genuine faith and ministry. This transformation empowers believers to share the gospel authentically.

Paul reminds us that the gospel's authority comes from God, not human institutions. This highlights the importance of divine revelation and the sufficiency of Scripture in guiding our faith and practice.

Paul's mission to the Gentiles teaches us about the inclusivity of the gospel. It challenges us to reach out beyond our comfort zones and cultural boundaries to share the message of Christ with all people.

Paul's Independent Ministry and Validation (17-20)

Paul further elaborates on his independent ministry and subsequent validation by the apostles in Jerusalem.

Independence from Jerusalem ...

Paul's decision not to go to Jerusalem to see the apostles soon after his conversion underlines his independence. The gospel he now preaches did not come from the apostles but directly from Christ. This independence is important because it emphasizes the divine origin of his message.

Paul did not need human endorsement to validate his apostleship; his authority came from Christ Himself. This independence also highlights the universality of the gospel. The message of salvation through Jesus Christ is not confined to a particular group or location but is meant for all people, everywhere. Paul's ministry to the Gentiles reveals the inclusive nature of the gospel, breaking down barriers and extending God's grace to all nations.

Visit to Peter and James ...

After three years, Paul went up to Jerusalem to get acquainted with Cephas (Peter) and stayed with him for fifteen days. He also saw James, the Lord's brother. This visit, though brief, provided an opportunity for mutual recognition and fellowship. It also demonstrated that Paul's gospel was in harmony with the message preached by the other apostles.

Paul's visit to Peter and James serves as an important moment of connection and affirmation. While his gospel was independent, it was not isolated. The fellowship and recognition by these key apostles validated Paul's ministry and highlighted the unity of the early church.

This visit also reveals the importance of relationships and collaboration in ministry, even as we maintain our distinct callings.

Integrity and honesty ...

Paul assures his readers that what he is writing is no lie, emphasizing his integrity and honesty. This assertion is important because it counters any accusations that Paul's gospel had been fabricated or was deceptive. His testimony is truthful and reliable, grounded in his personal encounter with Christ and consistent with the message of the other apostles.

Integrity and honesty are essential qualities in ministry. Paul's assurance of his truthfulness serves as a model for us today. In a world where trust is so often compromised, maintaining integrity and honesty in our words and actions is crucial for effective witness and ministry. Our lives should reflect the truth of the gospel we proclaim, demonstrating the transforming power of God's grace.

Paul's Ministry in Syria and Cilicia (Verses 21-24)

Paul concludes this section by describing his ministry in Syria and Cilicia and the response of the Judean churches.

Ministry in Syria and Cilicia ...

This region included his hometown of Tarsus, indicating that Paul returned to familiar territory to preach the gospel.

Paul's ministry in these areas was likely focused on establishing and then strengthening churches, as well as evangelizing both Jews and Gentiles. Paul's ministry in Syria and Cilicia highlights the geographical spread of the gospel at that time.

It was not confined to Jerusalem or Judea but extended to the broader regions of the Roman Empire. This expansion revealed the missionary nature of the gospel, which calls us to go beyond our comfort zones and reach people in diverse contexts with the message of Christ.

Unknown to the Judean Churches ...

Paul notes that he was personally unknown to the churches of Judea that are in Christ. They had not met him face to face but had only heard reports about him. This anonymity revealed the humility and focus of Paul's ministry. He was not seeking personal recognition or fame but was dedicated to preaching the gospel and serving Christ.

The churches in Judea only knew Paul by reputation, having heard the remarkable reports of his transformation and ministry. This serves as a reminder that our impact is not always measured by personal recognition but by the faithfulness of our witness and the fruit of our ministry. God can use our lives and testimonies to inspire and encourage others, even if we remain unknown to them.

Praise to God ...

The Judean churches praised God because of Paul. They heard the report: *"The man who formerly persecuted us is now preaching the faith which he once tried to destroy."* Paul's transformation and ministry were powerful testimonies to the grace and power of God.

The response of the Judean churches was not to elevate Paul but to give glory to God for His work in Paul's life. Paul's transformation from persecutor to preacher was a cause for praise and worship. It highlighted the power of God's grace to change lives and the truth of the gospel he proclaimed.

The response of the Judean churches reminds us that our ultimate goal in ministry is to bring glory to God. When people see the transforming work of God in our lives, their response should be to praise and worship Him.

Conclusion

As we reflect on Galatians 1:11-24, we are reminded of the divine origin and transformative power of the gospel. Paul's testimony reminds us that the gospel is not a human invention but a divine revelation, given by Jesus Christ Himself. It has the power to radically change lives, turning persecutors into preachers and opponents into advocates.

The Apostle Paul's life and ministry serve as a powerful example of God's grace and sovereignty. He was set apart from birth, called by grace, and transformed by the revelation of Christ. His independence from human authority and his immediate obedience to God's call demonstrate his unwavering commitment to the gospel of Jesus Christ.

In our own lives, we are called to embrace the gospel with the same passion and dedication. We are to guard its purity, proclaim its truth, and live out its transformative power. We should seek to please God above all, relying on His grace and power to fulfill the calling He has placed on our lives. May our lives, like Paul's, be a testimony to the grace and power of God, bringing glory to Him and advancing His kingdom.

3. UNITY IN THE GOSPEL

As we continue our exploration of the book of Galatians, in this chapter we will be looking at a passage which speaks of a critical moment in Paul's ministry and in the history of the early church. It details Paul's visit to Jerusalem and his meeting with the apostles to confirm the gospel he preached among the Gentiles. As we explore these verses, we will see the importance of unity in the gospel, the affirmation of Paul's ministry, and the agreement on the inclusion of the Gentiles without the requirement of adhering to Jewish law.

> **Galatians 2:1-10** *"Then after fourteen years, I went up again to Jerusalem, this time with Barnabas. I took Titus along also. I went in response to a revelation and, meeting privately with those esteemed as leaders, I presented to them the gospel that I preach among the Gentiles. I wanted to be sure I was not running and had not been running my race in vain. Yet not even Titus, who was with me, was compelled to be circumcised, even though he was a Greek.*
>
> *This matter arose because some false believers had infiltrated our ranks to spy on the freedom we have in Christ Jesus and to make us slaves. We did not give in to them for a moment, so that the truth of the gospel might be preserved for you.*
>
> *As for those who were held in high esteem - whatever they were makes no difference to me; God does not show favoritism - they added nothing to my message. On the contrary, they recognized that I had been entrusted with the task of preaching the gospel to the uncircumcised, just as Peter had been to the circumcised.*
>
> *For God, who was at work in Peter as an apostle to the circumcised, was also at work in me as an apostle to the Gentiles.*

James, Cephas and John, those esteemed as pillars, gave me and Barnabas the right hand of fellowship when they recognized the grace given to me. They agreed that we should go to the Gentiles, and they to the circumcised. All they asked was that we should continue to remember the poor, the very thing I had been eager to do all along."

The Context of Paul's Visit to Jerusalem (Verses 1-2)

Paul begins by recounting his visit to Jerusalem, which took place many years after his previous visit. This visit was significant for several reasons.

The timeline ...

Paul mentions that this visit occurred fourteen years after his first visit to Jerusalem, where he had met Peter and James (Galatians 1:18-19). The exact timing of these fourteen years is debated among scholars, but it is generally agreed that it includes the period of Paul's ministry in Syria and Cilicia. The long interval underscores that Paul's ministry was independent of the Jerusalem apostles, although not disconnected from the broader Christian community.

This timeline is crucial because it highlights the maturity and development of Paul's ministry. He had been actively preaching the gospel among the Gentiles for a considerable period before this meeting. His ministry was well-established, and the gospel he preached had already borne much fruit. This context sets the stage for the significance of the Jerusalem meeting.

Companions: Barnabas and Titus ...

Paul was accompanied by Barnabas and Titus. Barnabas was a respected leader in the early church and also a close companion of Paul.

His presence would have added credibility to Paul's mission. Titus, a Greek and an uncircumcised Gentile believer, represented the very issue at stake - whether Gentile converts needed to adhere to Jewish customs, such as circumcision. The inclusion of Titus in this delegation was very strategic but also symbolic. Titus was a living example of a Gentile who had come to faith in Jesus Christ without adopting any Jewish customs. His presence also underscored the central issue that Paul was addressing - the freedom of Gentile believers from the requirements of the Jewish law.

Purpose of the visit ...

Paul went to Jerusalem in response to a revelation. This indicates that his visit was divinely ordained and not merely a human decision. He met privately with the esteemed leaders - James, Peter (Cephas), and John - to present the gospel he preached among the Gentiles. Paul wanted to ensure that his work was not in vain and sought confirmation and unity regarding his mission. The private nature of this meeting emphasizes its importance and sensitivity.

Paul was not seeking public approval or debate but a mutual understanding and agreement with the key leaders of the Jerusalem church. His desire to confirm that he had not been running his race in vain reflects his concern for the integrity and unity of the gospel message.

The Issue of Circumcision and False Believers (3-5)

One of the central issues discussed during this visit was whether the new Gentile converts needed to be circumcised according to Jewish custom.

Titus as a test case …

Paul notes that Titus, a Greek, was not compelled to be circumcised. This decision was significant because it affirmed that Gentile converts were not required to adopt Jewish customs to be fully accepted as followers of Christ.

Accepting Titus as an uncircumcised believer was a clear statement against the legalistic demands of the Judaizers and a practical demonstration of the gospel's power to transcend cultural and religious boundaries. It highlighted the sufficiency of faith in Christ for salvation, apart from any additional requirements.

This decision was a pivotal moment for the early church, affirming the inclusion of Gentiles without the need for conformity to Jewish practices.

False believers and the threat to freedom …

Paul explains that the issue arose because some false believers had infiltrated their ranks to spy on the freedom they had in Christ Jesus and to make them slaves. These false believers, often referred to as Judaizers, insisted that Gentile converts must follow the Jewish law to be true Christians. Their presence and teachings threatened the freedom of the gospel by imposing legalistic requirements.

The term *"false believers"* highlights the insidious nature of their influence. These individuals were not merely misguided but were actively working to undermine the gospel's message of freedom and grace. Their insistence on circumcision and strict adherence to the Jewish law represented a fundamental misunderstanding of the gospel and a threat to its purity and power.

Preserving the truth of the Gospel ...

Paul and his companions did not give in to these demands for even a moment, so that the truth of the gospel might be preserved for the Galatians and for all believers. This steadfast refusal to compromise underlines the importance of maintaining the purity of the gospel message. Paul's resolve reminds us of the critical nature of this issue and his commitment to the truth of the gospel.

Preserving the truth of the gospel is an essential task for every generation of believers. The gospel is the power of God for salvation, and any distortion or addition to it undermines its effectiveness and leads people away from the true source of salvation. Paul's unwavering stance serves as a model for us today, calling us to guard the gospel's integrity and proclaim its message of grace and freedom with clarity and conviction.

The Affirmation of Paul's Ministry (Verses 6-8)

Paul then recounts the outcome of his meeting with the Jerusalem apostles and their response to his ministry.

No added requirements ....

He states that those who were held in high esteem - James, Peter, and John - added nothing to his message. This affirmation is crucial because it signifies that the leaders of the Jerusalem church did not impose any additional requirements on Paul's gospel. They recognized that his message was complete and aligned with the truth of the gospel. The phrase *"added nothing"* serves to highlight the sufficiency and completeness of the gospel Paul preached. It underscores that salvation is by grace through faith in Christ alone, without the need for additional works or adherence to the Jewish law.

This agreement among the apostles was a very powerful affirmation of the unity and consistency of Paul's gospel message.

Recognition of Paul's apostleship

The apostles recognized that Paul had been entrusted with the task of preaching the gospel to the Gentiles, just as Peter had been to the circumcised. This mutual recognition of their respective ministries revealed the unity and diversity within the early church. God had called and equipped Paul to reach the Gentiles, while Peter focused on the Jews.

The recognition of Paul's apostleship by the Jerusalem leaders was a significant validation of his whole ministry. It affirmed that his calling and mission were divinely ordained and supported by the broader Christian community. This recognition also highlighted the complementary nature of their ministries, with each apostle playing a vital role in the spread of the gospel.

God's work in both ministries …

Paul emphasizes that the same God who was at work in Peter as an apostle to the circumcised was also at work in him as an apostle to the Gentiles. This statement stresses the unity of their mission and the divine empowerment behind their work. It was not about individual efforts but about God's sovereign work through them.

The recognition of God's work in both ministries highlights the unity and diversity of the early church. It emphasizes that the gospel is for all people, regardless of their cultural or religious background. The same God who called and empowered Peter to reach Jews, also called and empowered Paul to reach the Gentiles.

This unity within diversity is a powerful testimony to the gospel's universal scope and transformative power.

The Right Hand of Fellowship and Agreement (9-10)

Paul concludes this section by describing the outcome of his meeting with the Jerusalem apostles and the agreement they reached.

The right hand of fellowship ...

James, Peter, and John, those esteemed as pillars of the church, gave Paul and Barnabas the right hand of fellowship. This gesture was a formal recognition of their partnership and mutual respect. It signified their agreement and unity in the gospel and their commitment to work together for the spread of the message.

The right hand of fellowship was a powerful symbol of unity and collaboration. It also represented their mutual recognition and support, affirming their shared mission and commitment to the gospel. This gesture underlined the importance of unity and partnership in the early church, setting an example for us today to work together in harmony for the advancement of God's kingdom.

Agreement on ministry focus ...

They agreed that Paul and Barnabas should go to the Gentiles, and they to the circumcised. This agreement acknowledged their distinct callings as well as the complementary nature of their ministries. It underscored the importance of reaching different people groups with the same gospel message. This agreement on ministry focus reflects the strategic nature of their mission. It recognized the unique callings and gifts of each apostle, allowing them to focus their efforts on specific target groups.

This division of labor was not a sign of division but of strategic collaboration, ensuring that the gospel would reach as many people as possible.

Remembering the Poor

The only additional request from the Jerusalem apostles was that Paul and Barnabas continue to remember the poor, something Paul was already eager to do. This emphasis on caring for the poor revealed the social dimension of the gospel and the importance of demonstrating God's love through acts of compassion and justice.

Remembering the poor was a key aspect of the early church's mission. It reflected the heart of the gospel, which calls us to love our neighbours and care for those in need. This commitment to social justice and compassion was an integral part of their witness, demonstrating the transformative power of the gospel in practical ways.

Lessons for Today

As we reflect on Galatians 2:1-10, several important lessons emerge for us today.

Unity in the Gospel …

The unity demonstrated by Paul and the Jerusalem apostles is a powerful reminder of the importance of maintaining unity in the gospel. Despite their different backgrounds and ministries, they recognized the same gospel and the same divine calling.

This unity is essential for the effectiveness of our witness and the advancement of God's kingdom. In our own context, we must strive for unity in the gospel, recognizing that we are all part of the same body of Christ.

This unity does not mean uniformity but a mutual recognition and respect for our diverse callings and gifts. By working together in harmony, we can more effectively reach the world with the message of Christ.

The freedom of the Gospel ...

Paul's refusal to compromise on the issue of circumcision underscores the importance of preserving the freedom of the gospel. The gospel sets us free from the burden of legalism and the demands of the law, offering us grace and freedom in Christ. This freedom is not a license to sin but a call to live in the fullness of God's grace and love. As believers, we must guard against any teachings or practices that seek to add to the gospel or impose legalistic requirements.

The gospel is sufficient in itself, and our salvation is by grace alone, embraced by faith alone in the finished work of Christ alone. Let us embrace and live out this freedom, demonstrating the transformative power of the gospel in our lives.

The importance of affirmation and accountability ...

Paul's meeting with the Jerusalem apostles highlights the importance of affirmation and accountability in ministry. While Paul's ministry was independent, it was not isolated. He sought and received affirmation from the broader Christian community, recognizing the value of mutual support and accountability.

In our own lives and ministries, we must seek out and value affirmation and accountability. Being part of a community of believers provides us with the support, encouragement, and accountability we need to grow and thrive in our faith.

We need to build and maintain relationships which foster mutual affirmation and accountability, strengthening our witness and ministry.

The call to remember the poor ...

The request to remember the poor highlights the social dimension of the gospel and the call to demonstrate God's love through acts of compassion and justice. Caring for the poor and marginalized is an integral part of our witness and a reflection of the heart of God. Social action is not the gospel – but it is one of the fruits of embracing the gospel.

As followers of Christ, we are called to actively engage in works of compassion and justice, caring for those in need and advocating for the vulnerable. This commitment to social justice is a powerful testimony to the transformative power of the gospel and a tangible expression of God's love.

Conclusion

As we reflect on Galatians 2:1-10, we are reminded of the importance of unity in the gospel, the freedom we have in Christ, the value of affirmation and accountability, and the call to remember the poor.

Paul's encounter with the Jerusalem apostles was a pivotal moment in the early church, affirming the unity and diversity of their mission and preserving the truth of the gospel.

Let us strive to maintain the unity of the gospel in our own lives and communities, embracing the freedom we have in Christ and working together to advance His kingdom. Let us seek out and value affirmation and accountability, building relationships that support and strengthen our faith.

Let us also commit to caring for the poor and marginalized, demonstrating the love of God through acts of compassion and justice. Let me finish with a story.

I want you to picture a small village divided by a wide, rushing river. On one side live the villagers who have been there for generations, rooted deeply in their traditions and way of life. On the opposite bank reside new settlers, people from distant lands with different customs and languages.

For years, the river had been a barrier, keeping the two communities apart. Attempts to bridge the gap had failed, and mistrust grew. However, in the heart of the village lived an old carpenter named Jonathan. Known for his wisdom and faith, Jonathan saw the division and longed for unity.

One day, Jonathan began to build a bridge across the river. It was a daunting task, but he believed that bringing the two communities together was worth every effort. As he worked, he prayed for guidance and strength, trusting that God would help him complete the bridge.

Word of Jonathan's project spread, and soon, people from both sides of the river came to watch. Some were skeptical, others curious, but a few were inspired. A young man from the settlers' side, named David, offered to help. Despite their different backgrounds, Jonathan welcomed him warmly.

Together, they labored day and night, slowly but surely bringing the two banks closer. As the bridge took shape, more villagers joined in. They brought tools, shared meals, and exchanged stories. The work became a symbol of hope and unity.

Finally, the bridge was completed. On the day of its unveiling, Jonathan stood in the middle of the bridge, welcoming villagers from both sides. They met with hesitation at first, but then with smiles and handshakes. The bridge had not only closed the physical gap but also began to heal the divisions in their hearts.

Jonathan shared with them the story of Paul's visit to Jerusalem in Galatians 2:1-10. Just as Paul sought to unite Jewish and Gentile believers, Jonathan had built the bridge to unite their village. He reminded them that in Christ, all barriers are broken down and we are called to live in harmony and love.

The bridge stood as a testament to what can be achieved when we work together in faith. It was a tangible reminder that, like Jonathan, we are all called to be bridge builders, bringing unity and peace through the love of Christ.

This story of Jonathan's bridge shows us the power of unity in Christ. As Paul and the apostles worked to unite believers from different backgrounds, so are we called to build bridges of understanding and love in our communities. Let us be inspired to reach out, break down barriers, and reflect the unifying power of the gospel in our lives.

4. STANDING FIRM

We now explore one of the more intense and revealing sections in Paul's letter to the Galatians: Galatians 2:11-21. In this passage, Paul recounts a confrontation with Peter in Antioch, addressing issues of hypocrisy and the truth of the gospel. This passage is crucial for understanding the full implications of the gospel for both Jewish and Gentile believers, and it challenges us to examine our own lives for consistency and faithfulness to the gospel.

> **Galatians 2:11-21** *"When Cephas came to Antioch, I opposed him to his face, because he stood condemned. For before certain men came from James, he used to eat with the Gentiles. But when they arrived, he began to draw back and separate himself from the Gentiles because he was afraid of those who belonged to the circumcision group. The other Jews joined him in his hypocrisy, so that by their hypocrisy even Barnabas was led astray. When I saw that they were not acting in line with the truth of the gospel, I said to Cephas in front of them all, "You are a Jew, yet you live like a Gentile and not like a Jew. How is it, then, that you force Gentiles to follow Jewish customs?"*
>
> *We who are Jews by birth and not sinful Gentiles know that a person is not justified by the works of the law, but by faith in Jesus Christ. So we, too, have put our faith in Christ Jesus that we may be justified by faith in Christ and not by the works of the law, because by the works of the law no one will be justified. But if, in seeking to be justified in Christ, we Jews find ourselves also among the sinners, doesn't that mean that Christ promotes sin? Absolutely not! If I rebuild what I destroyed, then I really would be a lawbreaker. For through the law, I died to the law so that I might live for God.*

I have been crucified with Christ and I no longer live, but Christ lives in me. The life I now live in the body, I live by faith in the Son of God, who loved me and gave himself for me. I do not set aside the grace of God, for if righteousness could be gained through the law, Christ died for nothing!"

The Confrontation in Antioch (Verses 11-14)

Peter's hypocrisy ...

Paul opposes Peter to his face because Peter was clearly wrong. Before certain men came, Peter used to eat with the Gentiles. However, when these men arrived, Peter began to draw back and separate himself from the Gentiles because he was afraid of those who belonged to the circumcision group.

This behavior was hypocritical because Peter had previously lived like a Gentile and enjoyed fellowship with them. Peter's actions reflect a deeper issue of fear and inconsistency. His withdrawal from eating with the Gentiles was driven by a fear of criticism from those who insisted on adhering to Jewish customs. This fear led him to compromise the truth of the gospel, which proclaims the unity of all believers in Christ, regardless of their ethnic or cultural backgrounds.

The influence on others

Peter's hypocrisy did not go unnoticed. The other Jews joined him in his hypocrisy, and even Barnabas was led astray. This influence underscores the responsibility of leaders to act consistently with the truth of the gospel, as their actions can lead others astray. Peter's behavior created considerable division and confusion within the community, undermining the message of the gospel.

The impact of Peter's actions on others also highlights the communal nature of the Christian faith. Our behavior affects those around us, especially those who look up to us for guidance and direction.

When leaders compromise on the truth of the gospel, it can lead to widespread confusion and division within the church. This incident serves as a sobering reminder of the importance of integrity and consistency in our witness.

Paul's public rebuke ...

When Paul saw that Peter and the others were not acting in line with the truth of the true gospel, he confronted Peter publicly. Paul's rebuke was direct and unambiguous: *"You are a Jew, yet you live like a Gentile and not like a Jew. How is it, then, that you force Gentiles to follow Jewish customs?"* This public confrontation was necessary to address the public nature of Peter's actions and their serious impact on the community.

Paul's willingness to confront Peter publicly demonstrates his commitment to the truth of the gospel and his considerable courage to address issues of hypocrisy, even when it involves a fellow apostle.

This confrontation specifically highlights the importance of accountability within a Christian community. When leaders or members of the church deviate from the truth of the gospel, it is essential to address these issues openly and honestly to preserve the integrity of the message.

Justification by faith, not by works (Verses 15-16)

Paul then transitions from recounting the confrontation to expounding on the doctrine of justification by faith.

The shared understanding of Jewish Christians …

Paul begins by stating that "we who are Jews by birth and not sinful Gentiles know that a person is not justified by the works of the law, but by faith in Jesus Christ." This shared understanding among Jewish Christians highlights their understanding that adherence to the law cannot justify anyone.

Justification, or being declared righteous before God, comes by grace and it embraced through faith in Jesus Christ. This statement reflects a fundamental truth of the gospel that transcends cultural and religious boundaries. It emphasizes that justification is based solely on faith in Christ, not on our efforts or adherence to religious laws. This truth was revolutionary in Paul's time and remains foundational for our understanding of salvation today.

Personal faith in Christ …

Paul continues, *"So we, too, have put our faith in Christ Jesus that we may be justified by faith in Christ and not by the works of the law, because by the works of the law no one will be justified."* Paul and other Jewish Christians had placed their faith in Christ, recognizing that justification could not be achieved through the law. This personal faith in Christ is essential for salvation.

The personal nature of faith underscores the individual response required for salvation to be experienced. Each person must place their trust in Christ, recognizing their inability to achieve righteousness through their efforts.

This faith is a personal commitment to rely on Christ's finished work for salvation, leading to a transformed life in Him.

The universal application ...

Paul's emphasis on justification by faith, not by works, applies universally to all believers, both Jews and Gentiles. The law's inability to justify highlights the need for a saviour and the sufficiency of Christ's sacrifice. This doctrine is central to the gospel and must be upheld without compromise.

The universal application of the doctrine of justification by faith underscores the inclusivity of the gospel. It breaks down barriers between different groups, emphasizing that all people, regardless of their background, can be justified through faith in Christ.

This truth challenges us to embrace the unity and diversity within the body of Christ, recognizing that we are all equal recipients of God's grace.

Addressing Potential Misunderstandings (Verses 17-18)

Paul anticipates the potential misunderstandings about justification by faith and addresses them directly.

Does justification by faith promote sin?

Paul raises a rhetorical question: *"But if, in seeking to be justified in Christ, we Jews find ourselves also among the sinners, doesn't that mean that Christ promotes sin? Absolutely not!"*

This question addresses the concern that justification by faith might lead to moral slackness or encourage sinful behaviour. Paul emphatically denies this notion, affirming that Christ does not promote sin. This concern reflects a misunderstanding of the gospel's transformative power.

Justification by faith does not lead to a permissive attitude towards sin; rather, it leads to a transformed life characterized by holiness and obedience to God. Paul's emphatic denial underscores the gospel's call to live in a manner worthy of our calling in Christ.

Rebuilding what was destroyed ...

Paul explains, *"If I rebuild what I destroyed, then I really would be a lawbreaker."* This statement highlights the inconsistency of returning to the law after embracing the gospel of grace. Rebuilding the law as a means of justification undermines the gospel and makes one a lawbreaker. Paul's argument underscores the complete futility of relying on the law for our righteousness.

This illustration emphasizes the need for consistency in our understanding and application of the gospel. Once we have embraced the truth of justification by faith, we cannot revert to legalistic practices without contradicting the gospel. This consistency is crucial for maintaining the integrity of our faith and witness.

The Law and the Gospel ...

Paul's distinction between the law and the gospel is critical for understanding the nature of salvation. The law reveals our sin and our need for a saviour, but it cannot save us. The gospel, on the other hand, offers the solution to our sin through the finished work of Christ. This distinction must be maintained to preserve the purity of the gospel message. Understanding the relationship between the law and the gospel is essential for a balanced and biblical view of salvation. The law serves an important purpose in revealing our need for a saviour, but it's the gospel that provides the remedy.

This understanding helps us to appreciate the full scope of God's redemptive plan and also the centrality of Christ's sacrifice.

Living by Faith in the Son of God (Verses 19-21)

Paul concludes this section by describing the transformative implications of the gospel for his own life.

Dying to the Law ...

Paul declares, *"For through the law I died to the law so that I might live for God."* This statement reflects Paul's recognition that the law's demands have been fully met in Christ. Through his union with Christ in His death, Paul has died to the law's condemnation and power, freeing him to live for God. Dying to the law signifies a radical shift in our relationship with God.

It means that we are no longer bound by the law's demands and condemnation but are free to live in the grace and power of the gospel. This freedom is not an excuse for sin but a call to live in obedience and devotion to God, empowered by His Spirit.

Crucified with Christ ...

Paul continues with one of the most profound statements in Scripture: *"I have been crucified with Christ and I no longer live, but Christ lives in me. The life I now live in the body, I live by faith in the Son of God, who loved me and gave himself for me."* This declaration encapsulates the essence of the Christian life - union with Christ in His death and resurrection. Being crucified with Christ signifies the end of our old, sinful nature and the beginning of a new life in Christ.

It means that His life and power now reside in us, enabling us to live a life of faith and obedience. Paul's personal testimony underscores the transformative power of the gospel and the intimate relationship we have with Christ.

Living by Faith ...

Paul's statement that he lives by faith in the Son of God emphasizes the ongoing nature of the Christian life. Faith is not a one-time event but a continuous trust and reliance on Christ.

This faith is rooted in the love of Christ, who gave Himself for us. Understanding and experiencing Christ's love is the foundation of our faith and motivates our obedience.

Living by faith in the Son of God involves daily dependence on His grace and power. It means trusting in His promises, following His guidance, and living in the reality of His presence. This life of faith is characterized by a deep, personal relationship with Jesus Christ, grounded in His sacrificial love for us.

The Grace of God

Paul concludes, *"I do not set aside the grace of God, for if righteousness could be gained through the law, Christ died for nothing!"* This final statement reinforces the absolute necessity of grace for salvation. Any attempt to achieve righteousness through the law nullifies the grace of God and undermines the purpose of Christ's death.

The grace of God is the foundation of our salvation and the basis of our relationship with Him. It is by grace that we are saved, sustained, and empowered to live the Christian life.

Understanding the grace of God is crucial for our spiritual growth and our daily walk with Christ. It humbles us, reminding us that our salvation is entirely the work of God's mercy and love, and it empowers us to live in a way that honors Him.

Practical Applications for Our Lives

As we reflect on Galatians 2:11-21, a number of practical applications emerge for our lives today.

Stand firm in the truth of the Gospel ...

Paul's confrontation with Peter underscores the importance of standing firm in the truth of the gospel. We must be vigilant in guarding the purity of the gospel message and be willing to confront any distortions or compromises.
This requires a deep understanding of the gospel and a commitment to its truth.

In our own lives, we can apply this by studying the Scriptures diligently, embracing sound teaching, and being part of a community of faith that upholds the truth of the gospel. When we encounter false teachings or behaviors that contradict the gospel, we should address them with love and firmness, just as Paul did.

Avoid hypocrisy and live consistently ...

Peter's hypocrisy serves as a warning against living inconsistently with the gospel. Our actions must align with our beliefs, and we should strive to live out the truth of the gospel in every aspect of our lives. This includes our interactions with others, our decisions, and our daily conduct.

Living consistently with the gospel means being honest, transparent, and humble. It means acknowledging our failures and seeking God's grace to grow in righteousness. By living authentically, we will always bear witness to the transformative power of the gospel and inspire others to follow Christ with integrity.

Embrace justification by faith ...

Paul's teaching on justification by faith is a foundational truth that we must embrace fully. Our righteousness before God is not based on our works or adherence to the law but on our faith in Jesus Christ. This truth frees us from the burden of legalism and empowers us to live in the grace and freedom of the gospel.

For us to embrace justification by faith, we must constantly remind ourselves of the sufficiency of Christ's sacrifice and the completeness of our salvation in Him. We should reject any attempts to earn God's favour through our efforts and instead rest in the finished work of Christ. This understanding should lead us to live with gratitude, humility, and a deep sense of security in God's love.

Live by faith in the Son of God ...

Paul's declaration that he lives by faith in the Son of God who loved him and gave Himself for him is a powerful reminder of the intimate relationship we have with Christ. Living by faith means trusting in Christ's presence, guidance, and power in our daily lives. We can live by faith by maintaining a close relationship with Christ through prayer, worship, and the study of His Word. By seeking His will in our decisions and relying on His strength in our challenges, we demonstrate our trust in Him. This daily dependence on Christ transforms our lives and enables us to reflect His love and grace to others.

Remember the grace of God ...

Paul's emphasis on not setting aside the grace of God calls us to continually remember and rely on God's grace. Grace is the foundation of our salvation and the source of our strength for living the Christian life.

We must never lose sight of the grace that has saved us and continues to sustain us. Remembering the grace of God involves regularly reflecting on the gospel, expressing gratitude for God's unmerited favor, and extending grace to others. It means recognizing that our worth and identity are found in Christ alone and living in the freedom and joy that His grace provides.

Conclusion

As we conclude our reflection on Galatians 2:11-21, we are reminded of the centrality of the gospel and the importance of living consistently with its truth. Paul's confrontation with Peter challenges us to stand firm in the gospel, avoid hypocrisy, and embrace justification by faith.

His personal testimony of living by faith in the Son of God inspires us to cultivate a deep, personal relationship with Christ and rely on His grace daily.

Let me close this chapter with a story.

In a small town nestled in the mountains, there was a bridge that spanned a large, rushing river. This bridge was not just any bridge; it was the only way for the town's residents to reach the nearby city where they worked, shopped, and visited doctors. For generations, this bridge had stood firm against all sorts of weather: storms, floods, and heavy snows. It was a lifeline for the community.

One spring, the river swelled more than it had in decades, and the old bridge was put to a severe test. Logs and debris hammered against its structure day and night. Watching from the banks, the townspeople were anxious; fearing the bridge may give way under the force of the river. So an engineer from the city came to inspect the bridge.

After a thorough check, he gathered the townsfolk to share his findings. He explained how the bridge was built on deep, strong foundations, designed to withstand even the harshest conditions. Despite its age and the ferocity of the river, the bridge was safe. It was designed to stand firm.

This bridge is much like our faith. In Galatians 2:11-21, we see a vivid example of standing firm in the faith through the confrontation between Paul and Peter. Peter, swayed by pressure from certain groups, began to withdraw and separate himself from the Gentile believers.

Paul, recognizing the danger of this hypocrisy to the truth of the gospel, confronted Peter publicly. He stood firm not for personal pride but for the truth of the gospel which proclaims that both Jew and Gentile are justified by faith in Christ, not by observing the law.

Like the bridge, Peter's actions could have weakened the very fabric of the church's unity and the purity of the gospel, just as a damaged bridge threatens the safety and well-being of a town. Paul's confrontation was about more than correcting a peer; it was a bold stand to protect the integrity of the gospel, reinforcing the deep, strong foundations of our faith.

When we face pressures - from society, from within our own circles, or even from within ourselves - to compromise on our beliefs or to live in a way that contradicts the truth of the gospel, we must remember the example of Paul.

We are called to stand firm, not on our own strength but on the foundation that is Christ Jesus. Just like the town's bridge, we are built on something unshakeable, something that can withstand any storm or flood.

So let us take heart and stand firm. Let the truth of the gospel be the solid ground under our feet, and let our lives reflect that stability to the world around us, just as surely as that bridge continues to connect the townspeople to everything they need.

5. FAITH NOT WORKS

As we continue to journey through Paul's letter to the Galatians, we come to chapter three, and today we will be looking at the first 14 verses. In this passage, Paul addresses the Galatians' foolishness in turning away from the gospel of faith to rely on the works of the law.

He reminds them of the power of faith in Christ and the futility of trying to earn God's favour through human effort. This message is vital for us today as it challenges us to examine the basis of our own faith and reliance on grace.

> **Galatians 3:1-14** *"You foolish Galatians! Who has bewitched you? Before your very eyes Jesus Christ was clearly portrayed as crucified. I would like to learn just one thing from you: Did you receive the Spirit by the works of the law, or by believing what you heard? Are you so foolish? After beginning by means of the Spirit, are you now trying to finish by means of the flesh? Have you experienced so much in vain - if it really was in vain?*
>
> *So again, I ask, does God give you his Spirit and work miracles among you by the works of the law, or by your believing what you heard? So also, Abraham "believed God, and it was credited to him as righteousness."*
>
> *Understand, then, that those who have faith are children of Abraham. Scripture foresaw that God would justify the Gentiles by faith and announced the gospel in advance to Abraham: "All nations will be blessed through you." So those who rely on faith are blessed along with Abraham, the man of faith. For all who rely on the works of the law are under a curse, as it is written: "Cursed is everyone who does not continue to do everything written in the Book of the Law."*

Clearly no one who relies on the law is justified before God, because *"the righteous will live by faith."* The law is not based on faith; on the contrary, it says, *"The person who does these things will live by them."*

Christ redeemed us from the curse of the law by becoming a curse for us, for it is written: *"Cursed is everyone who is hung on a pole."* He redeemed us in order that the blessing given to Abraham might come to the Gentiles through Christ Jesus, so that by faith we might receive the promise of the Spirit.

The Foolishness of the Galatians (Verses 1-5)

Paul begins this section with a strong rebuke to the Galatians, calling them foolish for turning away from the gospel of grace to rely on the works of the law.

Paul's rebuke ...

Paul opens with a sharp rebuke: *"You foolish Galatians! Who has bewitched you?"* This strong language indicates his deep frustration and concern. The term "bewitched" suggests that the Galatians have been deceived or charmed away from the truth.

Paul reminds them that Jesus Christ was clearly portrayed as crucified before their very eyes, emphasizing the centrality of Christ's sacrifice.

Paul's use of the word *"foolish"* conveys the seriousness of their error. It reflects not just a lack of understanding but a willful departure from the truth they once embraced. This strong rebuke serves as a wake-up call to the Galatians, urging them to reconsider their actions and return to the true gospel.

Receiving the Spirit ...

Paul asks a critical question: *"Did you receive the Spirit by the works of the law, or by believing what you heard?"* This rhetorical question underscores that the Galatians received the Holy Spirit through faith, not by adhering to the law.

Their initial experience of the Spirit was a result of believing the gospel message. The reception of the Holy Spirit is powerful evidence of God's work in a believer's life. It is not something that can be earned or achieved through human effort.

Paul's question highlights the contrast between the works of the law and the simplicity of faith. The Spirit's presence is a testimony to the sufficiency of Christ's work and the effectiveness of the gospel.

Foolishness of returning to the Law ...

Paul continues, *"Are you so foolish? After beginning by means of the Spirit, are you now trying to finish by means of the flesh?"* This question exposes the absurdity of starting with faith and then attempting to achieve spiritual maturity through human effort. Paul reminds them of their experiences and the miracles they witnessed, which were all the result of faith, not the law.

The Galatians' attempt to return to the law reflects a misunderstanding of the gospel's power and purpose. Paul's rhetorical question emphasizes the futility of relying on human effort after experiencing the transformative work of the Spirit. This challenge calls the Galatians to recognize their error and return to the foundational truth of faith in Christ.

Experiencing in vain ...

Paul asks, *"Have you experienced so much in vain - if it really was in vain?"* This question emphasizes the significance of their spiritual experiences and the risk of nullifying them by turning back to the law. Paul appeals to their past encounters with God's grace and the Spirit's work in their lives as a basis for rejecting the law's demands.

The potential of experiencing in vain reminds us of the importance of perseverance in the faith. Paul's question serves as a warning that the journey of faith is a continual reliance on God's grace, not a temporary phase that can be replaced by legalism. It challenges the Galatians to hold fast to the gospel and avoid the pitfalls of self-reliance.

Miracles and faith ...

Paul reinforces his argument by asking, *"Does God give you his Spirit and work miracles among you by the works of the law, or by your believing what you heard?"* The answer is obvious - God works through faith, not through the law. This statement underscores the ongoing nature of faith in the Christian life, as God's work continues to be manifested through belief, not human efforts.

The reference to miracles emphasizes the power and presence of God in the believers' lives. These miraculous works are a testament to the effectiveness of faith and the inadequacy of the law. Paul's question challenges the Galatians to recognize the source of God's work in their midst and to remain grounded in the gospel.

The Example of Abraham (Verses 6-9)

Paul uses the example of Abraham to illustrate the principle of justification by faith, not by works.

Abraham's faith ...

Paul quotes from Genesis 15:6: *"So also Abraham 'believed God, and it was credited to him as righteousness.'"* Abraham's righteousness was not based on his works but on his faith in God's promise. This example serves as a powerful argument for the principle of justification by faith.

Abraham's faith is a foundational example for us as we try to understand justification. His belief in God's promise was the basis for his righteousness, not his adherence to the law, which was given centuries later. This example reveals the timeless nature of faith as the means of receiving God's righteousness.

Children of Abraham ...

Paul explains, *"Understand, then, that those who have faith are children of Abraham."* This statement highlights the spiritual lineage of all believers. Those who have faith in Christ are considered true descendants of Abraham, regardless of their ethnic or cultural background.

Being children of Abraham emphasizes the inclusivity of the gospel. It transcends ethnic and cultural boundaries, uniting all believers in the family of God. This truth challenges any form of exclusivity or elitism within the church, calling believers to recognize their shared identity in Christ.

Scripture's foresight ...

Paul continues, *"Scripture foresaw that God would justify the Gentiles by faith and announced the gospel in advance to Abraham: 'All nations will be blessed through you.'"*

This reference to Genesis 12:3 shows that God's plan to justify the Gentiles by faith was revealed early in biblical history.

The foresight of Scripture reveals the continuity of God's redemptive plan. The promise to Abraham anticipated the inclusion of the Gentiles and the universal scope of the gospel. This understanding reinforces the consistency of God's purposes and the reliability of His promises.

Blessing through faith ...

Paul concludes, *"So those who rely on faith are blessed along with Abraham, the man of faith."* This statement affirms that the blessings promised to Abraham are extended to all who share his faith. Faith, not works, is the basis for receiving God's blessings.

The blessing through faith highlights the generosity and grace of God. It emphasizes that the same blessings promised to Abraham are available to all who believe, regardless of their background. This truth encourages believers to trust in God's faithfulness and to rely on His grace for their spiritual inheritance.

The Curse of the Law (Verses 10-14)

Paul then contrasts the blessing of faith with the curse of relying on the works of the law.

The curse of the Law ...

Paul states, *"For all who rely on the works of the law are under a curse, as it is written: 'Cursed is everyone who does not continue to do everything written in the Book of the Law.'"*

This quotation from Deuteronomy 27:26 highlights the impossibility of perfectly keeping the law and the resulting curse for failing to do so.

The curse of the law emphasizes the law's stringent demands and the impossibility of achieving righteousness through human effort. Only one human has ever walked this planet and perfectly obeyed the law of God – and that was Jesus of Nazareth. Paul exposes the futility of relying on the law for justification and underscores the need for a different means of salvation. This realization points to the inadequacy of legalism and the necessity of faith in Christ's life, death and resurrection.

Justification by faith …

Paul continues, *"Clearly no one who relies on the law is justified before God, because 'the righteous will live by faith.'"* This quote from Habakkuk 2:4 emphasizes that righteousness comes through faith, not through the law. Paul reinforces the principle that justification is based on faith alone.

The assertion that *"the righteous will live by faith"* highlights the centrality of faith in the believer's life. It affirms that true righteousness is not a result of human effort but a gift from God, received through faith. This truth challenges any reliance on works and calls believers to trust wholly in God's grace.

The nature of the Law …

Paul explains, *"The law is not based on faith; on the contrary, it says, 'The person who does these things will live by them.'"* This statement underscores the fundamental difference between the law and faith.

The law demands perfect obedience, while faith relies on God's grace. The nature of the law as a system of works contrasts sharply with the gospel's message of grace. While the law requires adherence to a set of rules, the gospel invites believers to trust in the finished work of Christ. This distinction is crucial for understanding the basis of our salvation and the nature of our relationship with God.

Christ's redemption...

Paul declares, *"Christ redeemed us from the curse of the law by becoming a curse for us, for it is written: 'Cursed is everyone who is hung on a pole.'"* This reference to Deuteronomy 21:23 highlights Christ's sacrificial death on the cross, where He took upon Himself the curse of the law on our behalf. Christ's redemption through His crucifixion is the heart of the gospel. It signifies the ultimate sacrifice, where Jesus took the penalty for our sins and liberated us from the curse of the law. This act of redemption underscores the depth of God's incredible love and the sufficiency of Christ's sacrifice for our salvation.

The blessing of Abraham ...

Paul concludes, *"He redeemed us in order that the blessing given to Abraham might come to the Gentiles through Christ Jesus, so that by faith we might receive the promise of the Spirit."* This statement highlights the purpose of Christ's redemption - to extend the blessing of Abraham to the Gentiles and to enable believers to receive the Holy Spirit by faith.

The blessing of Abraham through Christ underscores the inclusivity and generosity of God's plan. It affirms that the same blessings promised to Abraham are available to all who believe in Christ.

This truth highlights the unity and diversity within the body of Christ, where all believers share in the same spiritual inheritance.

Practical Applications for Our Lives

When reflecting on the first 14 verses of Galatians 3, several practical applications emerge for our lives today.

Embrace the simplicity of faith ...

Paul's rebuke of the Galatians challenges us to embrace the simplicity of faith in Christ. We must resist the temptation to add human effort or legalistic practices to the gospel. Our salvation and spiritual growth are rooted in faith, not in works. To embrace the simplicity of faith, we must focus on the core message of the gospel and rely on God's grace for our salvation. This involves a continual trust in Christ's finished work and a rejection of any attempts to earn God's favour through our own efforts. By keeping our faith simple and focused on Christ, we can experience the fullness of God's grace and live in the freedom He provides.

Live consistently with the Gospel ...

Paul's challenge to the Galatians to live consistently with the gospel calls us to examine our own lives for areas of inconsistency or hypocrisy. Our actions should align with our beliefs, and we should strive to live out the truth of the gospel in every aspect of our lives. Living consistently with the gospel involves a commitment to integrity and authenticity. It means allowing the truth of the gospel to shape all our attitudes, behaviours, and relationships.

By living in a manner that reflects our faith, we bear witness to the transformative power of the gospel and inspire others to follow Christ.

Recognize the futility of legalism ...

Paul's contrast between faith and the law underscores the complete futility of legalism. We must recognize that our righteousness before God can never be achieved through human effort or through adherence to religious rules. True righteousness comes through faith in Christ alone.

To recognize the futility of legalism, we must be vigilant in identifying and rejecting any legalistic tendencies in our own lives. This involves a continual reliance on God's grace and a rejection of any attempts to earn His favour through our works. By embracing the gospel of grace, we can experience the freedom and joy of living in God's love.

Reliance on the Holy Spirit ...

Paul's emphasis on receiving the Spirit through faith highlights the importance of relying on the Holy Spirit for our spiritual growth and empowerment. The Spirit's presence in our lives is a testimony to the effectiveness of faith and the inadequacy of the law.

Relying on the Holy Spirit involves cultivating a relationship with Him through prayer, worship, and obedience. It means seeking His guidance, listening to His voice, and allowing Him to work in and through us. By living in dependence on the Spirit, we can experience His power and presence in our daily lives.

Celebrate the inclusivity of the Gospel ...

Paul's teaching on the blessing of Abraham through faith emphasizes the inclusivity of the gospel. We must celebrate the unity and diversity within the body of Christ, recognizing that all believers, regardless of their background, are recipients of God's grace.

Celebrating the inclusivity of the gospel involves embracing the diversity within the church and seeking to build relationships with believers from different cultures and backgrounds. It means recognizing our shared identity in Christ and working together to advance His kingdom. By celebrating the inclusivity of the gospel, we reflect the heart of God and demonstrate the power of His love.

Conclusion

As we conclude our reflection on Galatians 3:1-14, we are reminded of the centrality of faith in the Christian life and the futility of relying on the works of the law. Paul's challenge to the Galatians to embrace the simplicity of faith, live consistently with the gospel, and rely on the Holy Spirit is a powerful message for us today.

Let us strive to live by faith in the Son of God, who loved us and gave Himself for us. Let us reject any attempts to earn God's favour through our efforts and instead rely on His grace for our salvation and our spiritual growth. May we celebrate the inclusivity of the gospel and work together to advance God's kingdom, reflecting His love and grace to the world.

6. THE PROMISE AND THE LAW

In the second half of Galatians 3, the Apostle Paul delves into the relationship between God's promise to Abraham and the Law given to Moses, explaining how both find their fulfillment in Christ. This text challenges us to understand the purpose of the Law, the nature of God's promise, and the unity we have in Christ.

> **Galatians 3:15-29** *"Brothers and sisters, let me take an example from everyday life. Just as no one can set aside or add to a human covenant that has been duly established, so it is in this case. The promises were spoken to Abraham and to his seed. Scripture does not say "and to seeds," meaning many people, but "and to your seed," meaning one person, who is Christ.*
>
> *What I mean is this: The law, introduced 430 years later, does not set aside the covenant previously established by God and thus do away with the promise. For if the inheritance depends on the law, then it no longer depends on the promise; but God in his grace gave it to Abraham through a promise.*
>
> *Why, then, was the law given at all? It was added because of transgressions until the Seed to whom the promise referred had come. The law was given through angels and entrusted to a mediator. A mediator, however, implies more than one party; but God is one. Is the law, therefore, opposed to the promises of God? Absolutely not! For if a law had been given that could impart life, then righteousness would certainly have come by the law.*
>
> *But Scripture has locked up everything under the control of sin, so that what was promised, being given through faith in Jesus Christ, might be given to those who believe.*

Before the coming of this faith, we were held in custody under the law, locked up until the faith that was to come would be revealed. So, the law was our guardian until Christ came that we might be justified by faith. Now that this faith has come, we are no longer under a guardian.

So, in Christ Jesus you are all children of God through faith, for all of you who were baptized into Christ have clothed yourselves with Christ. There is neither Jew nor Gentile, neither slave nor free, nor is there male and female, for you are all one in Christ Jesus. If you belong to Christ, then you are Abraham's seed, and heirs according to the promise."

The Unchanging Nature of God's Promise (Verses 15-18)

Paul begins this section by emphasizing the permanence and priority of God's promise to Abraham over the Law given to Moses.

The human covenant analogy ...

Paul uses an analogy from everyday life: *"Just as no one can set aside or add to a human covenant that has been duly established, so it is in this case."* Once a human covenant is confirmed, it cannot be altered or annulled. Paul applies this principle to God's covenant with Abraham, indicating that the promise made to Abraham is unchanging and irrevocable.

This analogy helps the Galatians, and us, to understand the permanence of God's promise. Human covenants, once ratified, are binding and secure, in spite of our fallen, sinful condition. How much more, then, is God's covenant, established by His word and character, unchangeable and reliable? This truth provides a foundation of assurance and trust in God's promises.

The promise to Abraham and his seed ...

Paul emphasizes the promises were spoken to Abraham and to his *"seed."* He points out that Scripture does not say *"and to seeds,"* meaning many people, but *"and to your seed,"* meaning one person, Who is Christ. This distinction highlights that the promise given to Abraham finds its ultimate fulfillment in Jesus Christ.

The focus on the singular seed points to the Christocentric nature of God's redemptive plan. All of God's promises to Abraham culminate in Jesus Christ, Who is the true heir of the promise. This interpretation affirms that the blessings promised to Abraham are accessible to all who are in Christ, making Him central to our faith and our eternal inheritance.

The Law and the promise ...

Paul clarifies, *"The law, introduced 430 years later, does not set aside the covenant previously established by God and thus do away with the promise."* The giving of the Law at Sinai did not nullify or replace the promise made to Abraham. The promise remains primary, and the Law cannot alter its terms. The temporal sequence of the promise and the Law is significant. The promise came first, establishing God's unchanging purpose. The Law, given centuries later, was not intended to replace the promise but to serve a different purpose. This understanding helps us see the continuity of God's plan and the distinct roles of the promise and the Law in salvation history.

Inheritance by promise, not by Law ...

Paul concludes, *"For if the inheritance depends on the law, then it no longer depends on the promise; but God in his grace gave it to Abraham through a promise."*

The inheritance promised to Abraham and his descendants is based on God's gracious promise, not on the observance of the Law.

This distinction is crucial for understanding the basis of our relationship with God. The inheritance we receive - eternal life, the blessings of the covenant, and the presence of the Holy Spirit - is grounded in God's grace and promise, not in our ability to keep the Law. This truth frees us from the burden of legalism and invites us to rest in God's grace.

The Purpose of the Law (Verses 19-22)

Paul then addresses the purpose of the Law and its relationship to the promise.

The role of the Law ...

Paul asks, *"Why, then, was the law given at all?"* He answers, *"It was added because of transgressions until the Seed to Whom the promise referred had come."* The Law was given to address sin and reveal its true nature, serving as a temporary measure until Christ, the promised Seed, arrived.

The Law's role in highlighting transgressions is essential for understanding its purpose. By exposing sin, the Law makes us aware of our need for a Saviour. It acts as a mirror, showing us our shortcomings and pointing us to Christ. This function of the Law is preparatory, leading us to the fulfillment found in Jesus.

The mediator and God's oneness ...

Paul notes that *"the law was given through angels and entrusted to a mediator. A mediator, however, implies more than one party; but God is one."*

The giving of the Law always involved intermediaries, emphasizing its indirect nature compared to the direct promise given to Abraham by God Himself.

The mention of the mediator highlights the difference in how the promise and the Law were given. The promise was given directly by God, underscoring its immediacy and personal nature. In contrast, the Law was mediated, indicating a degree of separation. This contrast reinforces the primacy of the promise over the Law.

The Law and God's promises ...

Paul asks, *"Is the law, therefore, opposed to the promises of God? Absolutely not!"* He explains that if a law could impart life, then righteousness would have come by the law. However, Scripture has "locked up everything under the control of sin, so that what was promised, being given through faith in Jesus Christ, might be given to those who believe."

The relationship between the Law and the promise is not one of opposition but of different roles. The Law cannot impart life or righteousness; it reveals sin and points us to our need for a Saviour. The promise, fulfilled in Christ, offers life and righteousness through faith. Understanding this, harmonizes the roles of the Law and the promise in God's redemptive plan.

The imprisonment under sin ...

Paul's phrase *"locked up everything under the control of sin"* illustrates the comprehensive nature of sin's power and the Law's role in highlighting it. The Law confines everybody under sin, revealing the universal need for redemption. This imprisonment under sin sets the stage for the liberating work of Christ.

Understanding our imprisonment under sin is essential for appreciating the gospel. The Law's exposure of sin and our inability to overcome it by our efforts magnifies the necessity and sufficiency of Christ's redemptive work. This perspective leads us to a deeper gratitude for God's grace and a clearer grasp of our dependence on Christ.

The Law as a Guardian (Verses 23-25)

Paul describes the Law as a guardian and explains its temporary role until the coming of Christ.

Custody under the Law ...

Paul states, *"Before the coming of this faith, we were held in custody under the law, locked up until the faith that was to come would be revealed."* The Law acted as a custodian, keeping us confined and protected, but also highlighting our need for the coming faith. The imagery of being *"held in custody"* under the Law conveys both protection and restriction. The Law provided moral and ethical guidance, but it also exposed our sinfulness and inability to achieve righteousness on our own. This dual role prepared us for the revelation of faith in Christ.

The Law as a guardian ...

Paul continues, *"So the law was our guardian until Christ came that we might be justified by faith."* The term "guardian" (Greek: *paidagogos*) refers to a tutor or custodian responsible for the care and discipline of a child. The Law served this function, guiding and disciplining us until Christ came.

The guardian role of the Law underscores its preparatory nature. Like a tutor, the Law provided instruction and correction, but its purpose was not to be permanent.

It was designed to lead us to Christ, where true justification is found. This perspective helps us see the Law's value and its limitations.

No Longer Under a Guardian

Paul concludes, *"Now that this faith has come, we are no longer under a guardian."* With the arrival of Christ and the revelation of faith, the Law's role as a guardian is fulfilled. Believers are now justified by faith and are no longer under the custodianship of the Law.

The end of the Law's guardianship signifies a new era in God's redemptive plan. Believers are now free from the constraints of the Law and live under the grace and guidance of the Holy Spirit. This transition then marks a significant shift in our relationship with God, characterized by freedom, faith, and the indwelling presence of Christ Himself, through the Holy Spirit.

Unity and Identity in Christ (Verses 26-29)

Paul concludes this section by highlighting the unity and identity of believers in Christ.

Children of God through faith ...

Paul declares, *"So in Christ Jesus you are all children of God through faith."* This statement affirms that faith in Christ makes us part of God's family. Our identity as God's children is based on our faith, not on our adherence to the Law. Being children of God through faith emphasizes the intimate and relational aspect of our salvation. We are not merely servants or followers; we are beloved sons and daughters of God. This identity shapes our relationship with God and our understanding of His love and grace.

Clothed with Christ ...

Paul continues, *"For all of you who were baptized into Christ have clothed yourselves with Christ."* Baptism symbolizes our union with Christ, and being clothed with Christ signifies our new identity and righteousness in Him.

Being clothed with Christ reflects the transformative nature of our union with Him. It signifies that we are covered by His righteousness and empowered to live in His likeness. This imagery challenges us to live out our new identity, reflecting Christ's character and values in our daily lives.

Unity in Christ ...

Paul proclaims, *"There is neither Jew nor Gentile, neither slave nor free, nor is there male and female, for you are all one in Christ Jesus."* This radical statement emphasizes the unity and equality of all believers in Christ, breaking down cultural, social, and gender barriers. The unity in Christ challenges any form of discrimination or division within the church.

It calls us to embrace the diversity within the body of Christ and to value each person as an equal member of God's family. This unity is a very powerful testimony to the transformative power of the gospel and the inclusive nature of God's kingdom.

Heirs according to the promise ...

Paul concludes, *"If you belong to Christ, then you are Abraham's seed, and heirs according to the promise."* Belonging to Christ makes us heirs of the promise given to Abraham, receiving the blessings of the covenant through faith. Being heirs according to the promise emphasizes our rich spiritual inheritance in Christ.

We are recipients of God's blessings, including eternal life, the indwelling of the Holy Spirit, and the assurance of His love and faithfulness. This inheritance shapes our identity and our hope, grounding us in the certainty of God's promises.

Practical Applications for Our Lives

In Galatians 3:15-29, we can discover a number of practical applications for our lives today.

Rest in God's promise ...

Paul's emphasis on the unchanging nature of God's promise challenges us to rest in the certainty of God's word. Our salvation and inheritance are based on God's gracious promise, not on our ability to keep the Law. This truth invites us to trust in God's faithfulness and to rest in His grace.

Resting in God's promise involves letting go of our attempts to earn God's favour and instead trusting in His unchanging word. It means finding peace and assurance in the certainty of His promises, knowing that they are grounded in His character and fulfilled in Christ.

Understand the purpose of the Law ...

Paul's explanation of the Law's role as a guardian helps us understand its purpose and limitations. The Law reveals our sin and our need for a Savior, but it cannot impart life or righteousness. This understanding helps us appreciate the value of the Law while recognizing its preparatory nature. Understanding the purpose of the Law helps us avoid legalism and embrace the grace of the gospel.

It reminds us that the Law serves to point us to Christ, where true justification and life are found. This perspective fosters a deeper appreciation for the gospel and a reliance on God's grace.

Embrace our identity in Christ ...

Paul's teaching on our identity as children of God through faith challenges us to embrace our new identity in Christ. We are no longer defined by our past, our failures, or our adherence to the Law. We are beloved children of God, clothed with Christ's righteousness and empowered by His Spirit. Embracing our identity in Christ involves living out our new identity in our daily lives.

It means seeing ourselves as God sees us and allowing His love and grace to shape our actions, attitudes, and relationships. This identity empowers us to live in freedom and to reflect Christ's character in all that we do.

Promote unity and equality ...

Paul's emphasis on the unity and equality of all believers in Christ challenges us to promote inclusivity and equality within the church. We are all one in Christ, regardless of our cultural, social, or gender differences. This unity calls us to value and respect each person as an equal member of God's family. Promoting unity and equality involves actively seeking to build inclusive and diverse communities.

It means breaking down barriers that divide us and fostering relationships that reflect the unity and love of Christ. By living out this unity, we bear witness to the transformative power of the gospel and the inclusive nature of God's kingdom.

Live as heirs of the promise ...

Paul's teaching on our inheritance in Christ challenges us to live as heirs of God's promises. We are recipients of God's blessings, called to live in the assurance of His love and faithfulness. This inheritance shapes our identity and our hope, grounding us in the certainty of God's promises. Living as heirs of the promise involves embracing our spiritual inheritance and allowing it to shape our lives.

It means living with confidence and hope, knowing that we are beloved children of God and recipients of His blessings. This perspective empowers us to live with purpose and joy, reflecting the love and grace of our Heavenly Father.

Conclusion

As we conclude our reflection on Galatians 3:15-29, we are reminded of the centrality of God's promise, the purpose of the Law, and the unity and identity we have in Christ. Paul's teaching challenges us to rest in God's promise, understand the role of the Law, embrace our identity in Christ, promote unity and equality, and live as heirs of God's promises.

May we be a people who live out these truths with integrity, standing firm in our faith and reflecting the love and grace of Christ in all that we do. Let us strive to maintain the unity of the body of Christ, working together to advance His kingdom and bring glory to His name.

7. NO LONGER SLAVES

As we continue our journey through the letter to the Galatians, we come to chapter four. In this chapter we will be looking at the first eleven verses, as Paul paints a vivid picture of the transition from slavery to being the children of God, emphasizing the transformative power of the gospel. He explains how, through Christ, we have been adopted as God's children and are no longer slaves to the elemental spiritual forces of the world. This message is essential for understanding our identity in Christ and the freedom we have as God's children.

> **Galatians 4:1-11** *"What I am saying is that as long as an heir is underage, he is no different from a slave, although he owns the whole estate. The heir is subject to guardians and trustees until the time set by his father. So also, when we were underage, we were in slavery under the elemental spiritual forces of the world. But when the set time had fully come, God sent his Son, born of a woman, born under the law, to redeem those under the law, that we might receive adoption to sonship. Because you are his sons, God sent the Spirit of his Son into our hearts, the Spirit who calls out, "Abba, Father." So, you are no longer a slave, but God's child; and since you are his child, God has made you also an heir.*
>
> *Formerly, when you did not know God, you were slaves to those who by nature are not gods. But now that you know God - or rather are known by God - how is it that you are turning back to those weak and miserable forces? Do you wish to be enslaved by them all over again? You are observing special days and months and seasons and years! I fear for you, that somehow, I have wasted my efforts on you."*

The Heir and the Slave (Verses 1-3)

Paul begins by illustrating the condition of an heir who is still underage, comparing it to that of a slave.

The underage heir ...

Paul states, *"What I am saying is that as long as an heir is underage, he is no different from a slave, although he owns the whole estate."* Even though the heir is the rightful owner of the estate, he has no practical access to its privileges and responsibilities until he comes of age. Before then, he is under the authority of guardians and trustees who manage his affairs.

This analogy highlights the temporary nature of the heir's status. While he is the future master of the estate, his current experience is one of restriction and discipline, similar to that of a slave. This situation is meant to be temporary, with a defined endpoint when he will fully step into his inheritance.

Slavery to the elemental spiritual forces ...

Paul continues, *"So also, when we were underage, we were in slavery under the elemental spiritual forces of the world."* The term *"elemental spiritual forces"* (Greek: *stoicheia*) refers to the basic principles or fundamental elements of the world. Before coming to faith in Christ, both Jews and Gentiles were in bondage to these forces, whether through the Law or through pagan practices. The reference to "elemental spiritual forces" underscores the universal nature of human bondage. Both Jews, bound by the Law, and Gentiles, bound by pagan religions and philosophies, were enslaved to systems that could not bring true freedom.

This bondage was characterized by a lack of spiritual maturity and an inability to access the full privileges of God's promise.

The temporary nature of the Law ...

Paul's comparison of the underage heir to a slave serves to highlight once again the temporary role of the Law. Just as the heir is under the control of guardians until the time set by his father, so the Law functioned as a guardian until the coming of Christ. This period of guardianship was meant to prepare God's people for the full realization of their inheritance in Christ.

Understanding the temporary nature of the Law helps us appreciate its role in God's redemptive plan. The Law was never intended to be the final solution but a preparatory stage leading to the fullness of time when Christ would come to fulfill God's promise.

The Fullness of Time and Redemption (Verses 4-5)

Paul now transitions to the pivotal moment in history when God sent His Son to redeem humanity.

The fullness of time ...

Paul declares, *"But when the set time had fully come, God sent his Son, born of a woman, born under the law."* The phrase *"the fullness of time"* indicates that God's redemptive plan was executed at the precise moment He had determined.

This timing reflects God's sovereignty and perfect wisdom in orchestrating the events of history. The fullness of time signifies the culmination of all of God's preparatory work through the Law and the prophets.

It was the appointed moment for the arrival of the Messiah, when all the conditions were ripe for the fulfillment of God's promise. This timing emphasizes God's control over history and His faithfulness in keeping His promises.

The incarnation of Christ ...

Paul emphasizes that God sent His Son, *"born of a woman, born under the law."* This dual description highlights both the divinity and humanity of Christ. He was fully God, sent from the Father, and fully human, born of a woman. Moreover, being born under the law, Christ subjected Himself to the same conditions as those He came to redeem. The incarnation of Christ is central to the gospel message. By becoming fully human, Jesus identified with our condition, experiencing the limitations and challenges of human life. By being born under the law, He fulfilled its requirements perfectly, enabling Him to redeem those who were under its condemnation.

Redemption and adoption. ...

Paul continues, *"to redeem those under the law, that we might receive adoption to sonship."* The redemptive work of Jesus Christ involves liberation *and* transformation. He redeemed us from the bondage of the law, purchasing our freedom through His sacrificial death. This redemption was not merely a release from slavery but also a transition to a new status as adopted children of God.

Adoption as sons and daughters signifies a profound change in our relationship with God. We are no longer slaves but beloved children, with all the rights and privileges that come with being part of God's family. This transformation is clear evidence of God's grace and the effectiveness of Christ's redeeming work.

The Spirit of Sonship (Verses 6-7)

Paul now explains the implications of our adoption, highlighting the role of the Holy Spirit in affirming our new identity.

The Spirit's presence ...

Paul states, *"Because you are his sons (and daughters), God sent the Spirit of his Son into our hearts, the Spirit who calls out, 'Abba, Father.'"* The presence of the Holy Spirit in our hearts is the evidence of our adoption and the guarantee of our inheritance. The Spirit's indwelling signifies our intimate relationship with God as our Father.

The cry of *"Abba, Father"* reflects the very deep, personal connection we have with God. The term *"Abba"* is actually an Aramaic word that conveys intimacy and affection, it's akin to *"Daddy"* in English. This a relationship which is characterized by trust, love, and a sense of belonging, and it's made possible through the work of the Holy Spirit.

From slavery to sonship ...

Paul declares, *"So you are no longer a slave, but God's child; and since you are his child, God has made you also an heir."* This statement encapsulates the profound transformation brought about by the gospel. We have moved from a state of slavery to sin and the law to being God's adopted children, enjoying our full inheritance in God's family.

This transformation has significant implications for our identity and our daily lives. As God's children, we are no longer defined by our past failures or by the constraints of the law. We are defined by our relationship with God, with all the privileges and responsibilities that come with being His heirs.

Heirs of God ...

Being an heir of God means that we are recipients of His promises and blessings. Our inheritance includes eternal life, the indwelling of the Holy Spirit, and the assurance of God's love and faithfulness. This inheritance shapes our identity and our hope, grounding us in the certainty of God's promises.

Living as heirs of God involves embracing our spiritual inheritance and allowing it to shape every part of our lives. It means living with confidence and hope, knowing that we are beloved children of God and recipients of His blessings. This perspective empowers us to live with purpose and joy, reflecting the love and grace of our Heavenly Father.

The Danger of Returning to Slavery (Verses 8-11)

Paul warns the Galatians against turning back to their former state of bondage.

The former slavery ...

Paul reminds them, *"Formerly, when you did not know God, you were slaves to those who by nature are not gods."* Before coming to faith in Christ, the Galatians were enslaved to false gods and pagan practices. This bondage was marked by ignorance of the true God and subjugation to powerless idols.

The reference to their former slavery highlights the futility and misery of life apart from God. The idols they served could not provide true freedom or fulfillment. This reminder serves as a contrast to the new life they have in Christ and a warning against returning to their former state.

Knowing God and being known by God ...

Paul continues, *"But now that you know God - or rather are known by God - how is it that you are turning back to those weak and miserable forces? Do you wish to be enslaved by them all over again?"* The shift from not knowing God to knowing Him - and more importantly, being known by Him - marks a fundamental change in their relationship with the divine.

Being known by God underscores the personal and relational nature of our salvation. It is not merely about intellectual knowledge but about a deep, intimate relationship initiated by God. This relationship is transformative, offering true freedom and purpose. Paul's question challenges the Galatians to recognize the folly of turning back to their former bondage.

Observing special days ...

Paul points out, *"You are observing special days and months and seasons and years!"* The Galatians were adopting Jewish ceremonial practices, believing that these observances would enhance their spiritual standing.

This return to legalistic practices was a huge step back – leading them right into bondage again, and contradicting the radical freedom they had been given in Christ.

The observance of special days reflects a reliance on external rituals rather than on the internal work of the Spirit. While such practices may have cultural or traditional significance, they cannot bring about true righteousness or spiritual maturity.

Paul's critique emphasizes the sufficiency of Christ's work and the futility of relying on legalistic observances.

Paul's c oncern...

Paul expresses his concern, *"I fear for you, that somehow I have wasted my efforts on you."* This heartfelt expression reveals Paul's deep pastoral care for the Galatians.

He is worried that their return to legalism might nullify the progress they have made in their faith journey. Paul's concern underscores the importance of perseverance in the faith.

The gospel is not merely the starting point of our journey but the foundation upon which we must build our entire lives – every single day. Returning to legalism or any form of bondage severely undermines the transformative work of the gospel and threatens our spiritual growth.

Practical Applications for Our Lives

As we reflect on these 11 verses in Galatians 4, several practical applications emerge for our lives today.

Embrace your identity as God's child ...

Paul's teaching on adoption challenges us to embrace our identity as God's beloved children. We are no longer slaves to sin or the law; we are sons and daughters of God, with all the rights and privileges that come with this new status.

Embracing our identity as God's children involves living out this truth in our daily lives. It means seeing ourselves as God sees us and allowing His love and grace to shape our actions, attitudes, and relationships.

This identity empowers us to live in freedom and to reflect Christ's character in all that we do.

Live in the freedom of the Gospel ...

Paul's warning against returning to slavery calls us to live in the freedom that the gospel provides. We must resist the temptation to rely on legalistic practices or external rituals for our righteousness and instead trust in the sufficiency of Christ's work.

Living in the freedom of the gospel involves a continual reliance on God's grace and the guidance of the Holy Spirit. It means rejecting any attempts to earn God's favour through our efforts – instead, always resting in the finished work of Christ. This freedom empowers us to live with joy, confidence, and purpose.

Cultivate Intimacy with God...

Paul's emphasis on knowing God and being known by God challenges us to cultivate a deep, personal relationship with Him. Our faith is not about adhering to a set of rules but about experiencing the transformative power of God's love and empowering presence in our lives.

Cultivating intimacy with God involves spending time in prayer, worship, and the study of His Word. It means seeking His guidance, listening to His voice, and allowing Him to work in and through us. This relationship is the foundation of our faith and the source of our spiritual growth.

Guard against legalism ...

Paul's critique of the Galatians' observance of special days serves as a warning against all legalism. We must be therefore be vigilant in identifying and rejecting legalistic tendencies in our own lives.

Our righteousness before God is based solely on God's grace and is embraced by faith in Christ and His finished work, not on our own performance or adherence to external rituals. Guarding against legalism involves a commitment to the truth of the gospel and a reliance on God's grace.

It means recognizing the sufficiency of Christ's work and rejecting any attempts to try and add to it. By embracing the simplicity of faith, we can experience the fullness of God's grace and live in the freedom He provides.

Persevere in the faith ...

Paul's concern for the Galatians' spiritual well-being challenges us to persevere in our faith journey. The gospel is not only the starting point but also the foundation upon which we must build our entire lives. We must remain steadfast in our reliance on Christ and avoid returning to any form of bondage.

Persevering in the faith involves a continual commitment to growth and maturity. It means staying grounded in the truth of the gospel, seeking the guidance of the Holy Spirit, and remaining connected to the community of believers. By persevering, we can experience the transformative power of the gospel and reflect Christ's love to the world.

Conclusion

As we conclude our reflection on Galatians 4:1-11, we are reminded of the profound transformation which the gospel brings. Through Christ, we have moved from a state of slavery to being a child of God, receiving the Spirit of God and becoming heirs of His promises.

Paul's teaching challenges us to embrace our identity as God's children; live in the freedom of the gospel; cultivate intimacy with God; guard against legalism; and persevere in our faith journey.

May we be a people who live out these truths with integrity, standing firm in our faith and reflecting the love and grace of Christ in all that we do. Let us strive to maintain the unity of the body of Christ, working together to advance His kingdom and bring glory to His name.

8. PAUL'S HEARTFELT PLEA

In the second half of chapter four of Paul's letter to the Galatians, the Apostle's tone becomes deeply personal and emotional. He pleads with the Galatians to remember their shared history and to resist the influence of false teachers. Paul's heartfelt message reveals his pastoral care and his deep concern for their spiritual well-being.

This particular passage challenges us to examine our own relationships within the body of Christ and to appreciate the importance of truth, love, and integrity in our spiritual journey.

> **Galatians 4:12-20** *"I plead with you, brothers and sisters, become like me, for I became like you. You did me no wrong. As you know, it was because of an illness that I first preached the gospel to you, and even though my illness was a trial to you, you did not treat me with contempt or scorn. Instead, you welcomed me as if I were an angel of God, as if I were Christ Jesus himself.*
>
> *Where, then, is your blessing of me now? I can testify that, if you could have done so, you would have torn out your eyes and given them to me. Have I now become your enemy by telling you the truth?*
>
> *Those people are zealous to win you over, but for no good. What they want is to alienate you from us, so that you may have zeal for them. It is fine to be zealous, provided the purpose is good, and to be so always, not just when I am with you. My dear children, for whom I am again in the pains of childbirth until Christ is formed in you, how I wish I could be with you now and change my tone, because I am perplexed about you!"*

Paul's Plea and Personal Appeal (Verses 12-14)

Paul begins this section with a heartfelt plea and a personal appeal to the Galatians.

Paul's plea for imitation ...

He says: *"I plead with you, brothers and sisters, become like me, for I became like you. You did me no wrong."* Paul is urging the Galatians to adopt his perspective and freedom in Christ. He reminds them of his own approach to ministry, where he became like them, embracing their culture to share the gospel effectively.

Paul's appeal to *"become like me"* is emphasizing his own example of living in the freedom of the gospel. He had set aside Jewish legalism to reach the Gentiles, demonstrating a life of faith and liberty in Christ. This call to imitation is not about his personal glorification but about encouraging the Galatians to live in the same freedom and grace that Paul has experienced.

Shared history and hospitality ...

Paul continues by recalling their shared history: *"As you know, it was because of an illness that I first preached the gospel to you, and even though my illness was a trial to you, you did not treat me with contempt or scorn. Instead, you welcomed me as if I were an angel of God, as if I were Christ Jesus himself."* He reminds them of the warm reception and hospitality they extended towards him despite his illness.

The Galatians' initial reception of Paul highlights their genuine love and acceptance. They welcomed him despite his physical condition, seeing beyond his illness to the message he was bringing them.

This recollection serves to remind the Galatians of their initial joy and openness to the gospel, contrasting it with their current confusion and division.

Illness as a catalyst ...

Paul's reference to his illness is significant. It was the very circumstance that led to his extended stay and opportunity to preach the gospel to them. This unexpected trial became a catalyst for their encounter with the transformative message of Christ.

Paul's own weakness and vulnerability became the means through which God's power and grace were displayed. This perspective challenges us to see how God can use all our weaknesses and trials for His own purposes. Paul's illness, initially a hindrance, became a doorway for the gospel. This reminds us that God's power is made perfect in our weakness and that He can use any situation for His glory.

Empathy and contextualization ...

Paul's decision to become like the Galatians was an act of empathy and contextualization. He adapted his approach to meet them where they were, understanding their culture and perspective to effectively communicate the gospel. This approach reflects a fundamental principle of mission and evangelism: understanding and adapting to the cultural context of those we seek to reach.

Empathy in ministry should always involve more than just understanding; it requires entering into the experiences and challenges of those we serve. Paul's example encourages us to build genuine relationships, to listen, and to engage with others in ways that respect and honour their context.

This approach not only makes the gospel more accessible but also demonstrates the love and humility of Christ.

The Change in the Galatians' Attitude (Verses 15-16)

Paul expresses his bewilderment at the dramatic change in the Galatians' attitude towards him.

The loss of blessing ...

Paul asks, *"Where, then, is your blessing of me now?"* He reflects on their initial enthusiastic reception and contrasts it with their current alienation. Paul had witnessed their deep appreciation and love, evidenced by their willingness to sacrifice for him: *"I can testify that, if you could have done so, you would have torn out your eyes and given them to me."*

The loss of their initial blessing and joy is a poignant reminder of how easily relationships can be strained and distorted by external influences. Paul's question highlights the drastic shift from their previous joy and gratitude to their current estrangement. This change clearly shows us the impact of false teaching and the resulting confusion and division.

The cost of truth-telling ...

Paul confronts the difficult reality: *"Have I now become your enemy by telling you the truth?"* This rhetorical question highlights the painful truth that sometimes, speaking the truth can strain our relationships. Paul's commitment to the gospel and his responsibility to correct the errors of the Galatians, put him at odds with them. This tension reflects a common challenge in pastoral ministry and relationships within the church.

The truth can be uncomfortable and challenging, but it is essential for spiritual growth and integrity. Paul's willingness to risk his relationship with the Galatians for the sake of truth demonstrates his deep love and commitment to their spiritual well-being.

The importance of truth ...

Paul's question about becoming an enemy by telling the truth, highlights the important role that truth plays in our spiritual lives. Truth is foundational to our relationship with God and each other.

Without truth, our faith becomes unstable and susceptible to false teaching and deception. Embracing the truth involves a commitment to honesty and integrity. It means being willing to confront uncomfortable realities and to accept correction when necessary. This commitment to truth is essential for spiritual growth and maturity, and it fosters a community where trust and authenticity can flourish.

The challenge of correction ...

Paul's experience with the Galatians also illustrates the challenge of giving and receiving correction. Correction, though necessary, is often difficult to accept, especially when it challenges deeply held beliefs or behaviours. However, it is through correction that we grow and become more aligned with God's will. Receiving correction requires humility and openness to change. It means recognizing that we are not perfect and that we need others to help us see our blind spots. Giving correction requires wisdom, love, and a desire for the other person's growth and well-being. By embracing correction, we allow God to refine us and to transform us more into the likeness of Christ.

The Danger of False Zeal (Verses 17-18)

Paul warns the Galatians about the motives and tactics of the false teachers who are leading them astray.

Manipulative zeal ...

Paul exposes the motives of the false teachers: *"Those people are zealous to win you over, but for no good. What they want is to alienate you from us, so that you may have zeal for them."* The false teachers were using their zeal to manipulate the Galatians, not for their benefit but to create a following for themselves.

The false teachers' zeal was self-serving, aiming to create division and establish their own influence. Paul's exposure of their motives highlights the danger of being swayed by charisma and persuasive rhetoric without discerning the true intent. This warning challenges us to be vigilant and discerning, ensuring that our leaders and influencers are motivated by genuine love and truth.

Good zeal vs. misguided zeal ...

Paul continues, *"It is fine to be zealous, provided the purpose is good, and to be so always, not just when I am with you."* Paul acknowledges the value of zeal but emphasizes that it must be directed towards good purposes and should always be rooted in truth. Genuine zeal for the gospel and for God's kingdom is commendable, but misguided zeal can lead to division and error.

This distinction between good and misguided zeal calls us to evaluate our own passions and motivations. Are we zealous for the right reasons? Is our zeal based on truth and love, or is it driven by selfish ambition and divisive agendas?

Paul's counsel encourages us to cultivate a zeal that is grounded in the gospel and directed towards building up the body of Christ.

Discernment in leadership ...

Paul's warning about the false teachers emphasizes the need for discernment in choosing our leaders and influencers. We must look beyond charisma and persuasive speech to examine the character and motives of those we follow. True leaders are those who seek to serve and build up the body of Christ, not those who seek personal gain or influence.

Discernment in leadership involves a commitment to Scripture and a reliance on the Holy Spirit. It means seeking leaders who demonstrate humility, integrity, and a genuine love for God and His people. By choosing our leaders wisely, we can protect ourselves from harmful influences and ensure that we are being guided in truth.

The role of zeal in the Christian life ...

Paul's acknowledgment of good zeal reminds us of the importance of passion and enthusiasm in our Christian walk. Zeal, when directed towards good purposes, can be a powerful force for advancing God's kingdom and encouraging others in their faith. However, zeal must be grounded in truth and always motivated by love. Cultivating good zeal involves a deep commitment to God and His purposes. It means being passionate about the gospel, eager to share it with others, and dedicated to living out its truths in our daily lives. By aligning our zeal with God's will, we can make a significant impact for His kingdom and inspire others to do the same.

Paul's Deep Concern and Pastoral Heart (Verses 19-20)

Paul's pastoral heart is evident as he expresses his deep concern and longing for the Galatians.

Spiritual childbirth ...

Paul uses a powerful metaphor to describe his concern: *"My dear children, for whom I am again in the pains of childbirth until Christ is formed in you."* This imagery of childbirth conveys the intensity and depth of Paul's care and concern. Just as childbirth is a process of pain leading to new life, Paul's labour is directed towards the spiritual formation of the Galatian believers.

The metaphor of childbirth highlights the ongoing nature of spiritual growth and discipleship. Paul is not content with a superficial commitment; he longs to see Christ fully formed in them.

This process involves both struggle and perseverance, reflecting the deep investment required in pastoral care and spiritual mentorship.

Desire for personal presence ...

Paul expresses his longing to be with them: *"How I wish I could be with you now and change my tone, because I am perplexed about you!"* Paul's desire for personal presence reinforces his genuine care and the limitations of written communication. He wishes he could be with them to address their issues directly and to offer his guidance and support in person.

This longing for personal presence reflects the importance of relationship and face-to-face interaction in pastoral care.

While letters and messages can be able to convey truth and encouragement, there is no real substitute for the personal presence of a shepherd who can offer guidance, support, and correction in a loving and relational context.

The pain of spiritual leadership ...

Paul's metaphor of childbirth also reveals the pain and struggle inherent in spiritual leadership. Just as childbirth involves intense labour and pain, so does the process of guiding others in their spiritual journey. Paul's willingness to endure this pain reflects his deep love and commitment to the spiritual growth of the Galatians.

The pain of spiritual leadership is a reality that many pastors and leaders experience. It involves bearing the burdens of others, facing criticism and opposition, and persevering through challenges.

This pain, however, is accompanied by the joy of seeing lives transformed and Christ being formed in others. Paul's example encourages us to always embrace the challenges of spiritual leadership today with love and perseverance.

The goal of spiritual formation ...

Paul's ultimate goal is for Christ to be formed in the Galatian believers. This goal reflects the essence of discipleship: manifesting the life of Christ in our character, attitude, and behaviour. Spiritual formation is not about outward conformity, it's all about inward transformation that reflects and reveals the life of Christ in us.

The goal of spiritual formation calls us to focus on our own growth in Christlikeness. It involves a daily commitment to seek God, to surrender to His will, and to allow the Holy Spirit to work in us.

By prioritizing spiritual formation, we can experience the fullness of life that God intends for us and become effective witnesses for His kingdom.

Practical Applications for Our Lives

How then shall we live today in light of the teaching of Galatians 4:12-20? Several practical applications emerge.

Cultivate genuine relationships ...

Paul's deep concern and personal appeal to the Galatians highlight the importance of always cultivating genuine relationships within the body of Christ. Relationships built on trust, love, and mutual respect are essential for spiritual growth and accountability.

Cultivating genuine relationships involves investing time and effort in getting to know one another, sharing our lives, and supporting each other in our faith journeys. It means being honest and vulnerable, willing to offer and receive correction in a spirit of love. These relationships are the foundation of a healthy and vibrant church community.

Value truth and integrity ...

Paul's commitment to truth, even at the risk of straining his relationship with the Galatians, challenges us to value truth and integrity in our own lives. The gospel calls us to live in the light, being honest with ourselves and others about our struggles, failures, and our need for God's grace.

Valuing truth and integrity involves a commitment to personal and communal accountability. It means being willing to speak the truth in love, even when it is uncomfortable or challenging.

By prioritizing truth and integrity, we can foster a culture of authenticity and growth within our church community.

Discern motives and influences ...

Paul's warning about the false teachers' manipulative zeal calls us to discern the motives and influences in our own lives. We must be vigilant in evaluating the leaders, teachers, and influencers we follow, ensuring that their motives are aligned with the gospel and their teachings are rooted in truth.

Discerning motives and influences involves developing a deep knowledge of Scripture and a sensitivity to the Holy Spirit. It means being critical thinkers, not easily swayed by charisma or by clever, persuasive rhetoric. By cultivating discernment, we can protect ourselves and our community from harmful influences and false teachings.

Commit to spiritual growth ...

Paul's metaphor of childbirth and his longing for Christ to be formed in the Galatians challenge us to commit to our own spiritual growth. Spiritual formation is an ongoing process that requires intentional effort, perseverance, and a willingness to be shaped by God's Spirit, each and every day.

Committing to spiritual growth involves engaging in regular practices of prayer, Bible study, worship, and fellowship. It means being open to the guidance and correction of the Holy Spirit and seeking out opportunities for learning and discipleship. By committing to spiritual growth, we can experience the transformative power of the gospel and become more like Christ.

Appreciate the importance of pastoral care ...

Paul's deep concern and pastoral heart also remind us of the importance of pastoral care in the life of the church. Pastors and leaders play a crucial role in guiding, nurturing, and supporting the spiritual growth of the congregation. Their presence, teaching, and encouragement are vital for the health and vitality of the church. Appreciating the role of pastoral care involves supporting and praying for our pastors and leaders, recognizing the challenges and responsibilities they bear. It means being receptive to their guidance and correction and valuing their investment in our spiritual well-being.

However, pastoral care is the responsibility of every believer. Pastors and leaders are there to teach, guide and encourage us, but every member of our Church family has the responsibility to reach out to those around them and offer their love, support and encouragement. By fostering a culture of appreciation and pastoral care, we can strengthen the overall health of our church community.

Embrace empathy and contextualization ...

Paul's decision to become like the Galatians was an act of empathy and contextualization. He adapted his approach to meet them where they were, understanding their culture and perspective to effectively communicate the gospel. This approach reflects a basic principle of mission work and evangelism: understanding and adapting to the cultural context of those we seek to reach.

Empathy in ministry involves more than understanding; it requires entering into the experiences and challenges of those we serve. Paul's example encourages us to build genuine relationships, to listen, and to engage with others in ways that respect and honor their context.

This approach not only makes the gospel more accessible but also demonstrates the love and humility of Christ.

Persevere in difficult conversations …

Paul's willingness to risk his relationship with the Galatians for the sake of truth demonstrates the importance of persevering in difficult conversations. These conversations, though challenging, are essential for growth and alignment with God's will.

Persevering in difficult conversations requires courage, wisdom, and a commitment to love. It means being willing to address uncomfortable topics and to speak the truth with grace. By engaging in these conversations, we can foster a culture of growth and integrity within our church community.

Conclusion

As we conclude our reflection on Galatians 4:12-20, we are reminded of the depth of Paul's pastoral care and his commitment to the truth of the gospel. Paul's plea to the Galatians to remember their shared history, his warning against the influence of false teachers, and his longing for their spiritual growth challenge us to examine our own relationships within the body of Christ and to appreciate the importance of truth, love, and integrity in our spiritual journey.

May we be a people who cultivate genuine relationships, value truth and integrity, discern motives and influences, commit to spiritual growth, and appreciate the role of pastoral care. By living out these principles, we can experience the transformative power of the gospel and reflect the love and grace of Christ in all that we do.

9. FREEDOM IN CHRIST

In our study of Paul's epistle to the Galatians, we come now to Galatians 4:21-31. In this passage, Paul uses the story of Hagar and Sarah as an allegory to illustrate the difference between living under the law and living in the freedom of God's promise. This text is rich with theological insights and practical implications for our lives today.

> **Galatians 4:21-31** *"Tell me, you who want to be under the law, are you not aware of what the law says? For it is written that Abraham had two sons, one by the slave woman and the other by the free woman. His son by the slave woman was born according to the flesh, but his son by the free woman was born as the result of a divine promise.*
>
> *These things are being taken figuratively: The women represent two covenants. One covenant is from Mount Sinai and bears children who are to be slaves: This is Hagar. Now Hagar stands for Mount Sinai in Arabia and corresponds to the present city of Jerusalem, because she is in slavery with her children. But the Jerusalem that is above is free, and she is our mother. For it is written: "Be glad, barren woman, you who never bore a child; shout for joy and cry aloud, you who were never in labor; because more are the children of the desolate woman than of her who has a husband."*
>
> *Now you, brothers and sisters, like Isaac, are children of promise. At that time the son born according to the flesh persecuted the son born by the power of the Spirit. It is the same now. But what does Scripture say? "Get rid of the slave woman and her son, for the slave woman's son will never share in the inheritance with the free woman's son." Therefore, brothers and sisters, we are not children of the slave woman, but of the free woman."*

Understanding the Allegory (Verses 21-24)

Paul begins by challenging those who desire to be under the law, asking if they truly understand what the law says.

Two sons, two mothers ...

He references the story of Abraham's two sons: Ishmael, born to Hagar, the slave woman, and Isaac, born to Sarah, the free woman. He sets up a contrast between the two sons to illustrate two different ways of relating to God.

The story of Abraham's two sons would have been well-known to Paul's readers. Ishmael, the son of Hagar, was born according to human effort, as a result of Abraham and Sarah's attempt to fulfill God's promise through their own means. Isaac, on the other hand, was born according to God's promise, a miraculous birth given to Sarah in her old age. This contrast sets the stage for Paul's allegory.

Born according to the flesh vs. born according to the promise ...

Paul explains that Ishmael was born *"according to the flesh,"* while Isaac was born *"as the result of a divine promise."* This distinction highlights the difference between human effort and divine initiative. Ishmael represents what can be achieved through human means, while Isaac represents what can only be accomplished by God's power.

This distinction is crucial for understanding Paul's whole argument. Those who rely on the law are represented by Ishmael, as they try to achieve righteousness through human effort. In contrast, those who rely on God's promise are like Isaac, showing that righteousness is a gift through faith.

This sets up the broader theme of the passage: the difference between living under the law and living by faith in God's promise.

Two covenants ...

Paul then takes the story figuratively, stating that the two women represent two covenants. Hagar represents the old covenant from Mount Sinai, which leads to slavery, while Sarah represents the new covenant of grace, which leads to freedom.

By using the story of Hagar and Sarah, Paul illustrates the difference between the old covenant of the law and the new covenant of grace. The old covenant, given at Mount Sinai, is characterized by rules and regulations that lead only to bondage. The new covenant, established through Jesus Christ, is characterized by grace and freedom. This allegory helps Paul's readers understand the profound shift that has taken place in God's redemptive plan.

The present Jerusalem vs. the Jerusalem above ...

Paul contrasts *"the present city of Jerusalem,"* representing those under the law and in slavery, with *"the Jerusalem that is above,"* which represents the freedom of those who are under the new covenant.

The present Jerusalem symbolizes the physical and earthly realm of human effort and religious legalism. It is bound by the limitations of the law and human imperfection. By contrast, the Jerusalem 'above' symbolizes the heavenly and spiritual realm of divine grace and freedom. It is characterized by the fulfillment of God's promise and the transformative power of the Holy Spirit.

This contrast emphasizes the superior nature of the new covenant and the freedom it brings.

The Implications of the Allegory (Verses 25-27)

Paul further develops the implications of this allegory, focusing on the freedom which comes from being children of the promise.

Hagar and Mount Sinai ...

Paul states that Hagar represents Mount Sinai in Arabia and corresponds to the present city of Jerusalem, which is in slavery with her children. This statement underscores the bondage of those who attempt to rely on the law for their righteousness.

Hagar's representation of Mount Sinai highlights the connection between the law and slavery. Just as Hagar was a slave, so too are those who seek to be justified by the law. The present city of Jerusalem, bound by the law, was in a state of spiritual bondage. This imagery reinforces the futility of trying to achieve righteousness through human effort and legalistic practices.

The Jerusalem above ...

In contrast, Paul describes *"the Jerusalem that is above"* as free and our mother. This heavenly Jerusalem represents the community of believers who are under the new covenant of grace.

The Jerusalem above symbolizes the heavenly city of God, where His grace and freedom reign. It is the true home of believers, who are no longer bound by the law but live in the freedom of God's promise.

This imagery reminds believers of their true identity and inheritance as children of God. They are not slaves of an earthly realm of bondage but free in the heavenly kingdom of grace.

The barren woman rejoices ...

Paul quotes Isaiah 54:1, *"Be glad, barren woman, you who never bore a child; shout for joy and cry aloud, you who were never in labor; because more are the children of the desolate woman than of her who has a husband."* This prophecy speaks of the miraculous work of God in bringing life and fruitfulness where there was once barrenness.

The quote from Isaiah highlights the miraculous and gracious nature of God's work. Just as Sarah, who was barren, became the mother of many through God's promise, so too does the desolate woman rejoice because of God's intervention. This prophecy points to the inclusivity and expansiveness of God's promise. It brings hope and assurance that God can bring life and fulfillment where there once was none.

Children of Promise (Verses 28-31)

Paul is applying this allegory directly to the Galatians, emphasizing their identity as children of the promise.

Like Isaac, children of promise ...

Paul declares, *"Now you, brothers and sisters, like Isaac, are children of promise."* By faith in Christ, the Galatians are not children of slavery but of promise. This identity shapes their relationship with God and their understanding of their inheritance. Being children of promise means that all believers are part of God's redemptive plan, not because of our efforts but because of His grace.

Like Isaac, our birth is also miraculous; a result of God's intervention and promise. This identity frees us from the bondage of the law and assures us of our place in God's family.

Persecution from the children of the flesh ...

Paul notes that "at that time the son born according to the flesh persecuted the son born by the power of the Spirit. It is the same now." Just as Ishmael persecuted Isaac, so too do those who rely on the law persecute those who live by the Spirit. This persecution highlights the ongoing conflict between legalism and grace.

Those who rely on human effort often oppose those who live by faith, creating tension and division. Paul's observation serves as a warning to the Galatians about the nature of this conflict and encourages them to stand firm in their identity as children of promise.

Get rid of the slave woman and her son ...

Paul quotes Genesis 21:10, *"Get rid of the slave woman and her son, for the slave woman's son will never share in the inheritance with the free woman's son."*

This instruction underscores the need to separate from the old covenant of the law and fully embrace the new covenant of grace. The command to get rid of the slave woman and her son symbolizes the need to reject legalism and the bondage of the law.

Just as Hagar and Ishmael were sent away, so too must believers distance themselves from any system that seeks to justify them by human effort. This separation is necessary to fully embrace the freedom and inheritance that can only come through faith in Christ.

Not children of the slave woman, but of the free woman ...

Paul concludes, *"Therefore, brothers and sisters, we are not children of the slave woman, but of the free woman."* This declaration affirms the Galatians' identity and inheritance as children of the promise, living in the freedom of God's grace. This affirmation of identity is crucial for the Galatians and for us today. Believers are not bound by the limitations and bondage of the law; they are free, living under the grace and promise of God. This freedom shapes their relationship with God, their understanding of their inheritance, and their daily lives.

Practical Applications for Our Lives

As we reflect on Galatians 4:21-31, several practical applications emerge for our lives today.

Embrace your identity as children of promise...

Paul's teaching challenges us to embrace our identity as children of promise. We are not defined by our efforts or adherence to the law but by God's promise and grace. This identity shapes our relationship with God and gives us confidence in our inheritance. Embracing our identity as children of promise involves living out this truth in our daily lives. It means seeing ourselves as God sees us and allowing His grace to shape our actions, attitudes, and relationships. This identity empowers us to live in freedom and to reflect Christ's character in all that we do.

Reject legalism and embrace grace ...

Paul's allegory emphasizes the futility of legalism and the bondage it brings. We must reject any system that seeks to justify us by our efforts and instead embrace the grace that comes through faith in Christ.

Rejecting legalism involves a commitment to living by faith and relying on God's grace. It means letting go of the need to earn God's favour and trusting in the sufficiency of Christ's work. By embracing grace, we can experience the freedom and joy that come from being in a right relationship with God.

Stand firm in the face of persecution ...

Paul's observation about the persecution of the children of promise by the children of the flesh reminds us that living by faith can bring opposition. We must stand firm in our identity and trust in God's promise, even in the face of persecution.

Standing firm in the face of persecution involves a commitment to truth and a reliance on God's strength. It means being willing to endure hardship for the sake of the gospel and trusting that God will sustain us. By standing firm, we can bear witness to the transformative power of God's grace.

Celebrate the freedom of the New Covenant ...

Paul's contrast between the old and new covenants highlights the freedom that comes from living under the new covenant of grace. We must celebrate this freedom and live in the joy and assurance it brings. Celebrating the freedom of the new covenant involves a daily commitment to living in the light of God's grace.

It means embracing the transformative power of the Holy Spirit and allowing Him to guide our lives. By celebrating this freedom, we can experience the fullness of life that God intends for us.

Cultivate a community of grace …

Paul's teaching encourages us to cultivate a community of grace within the body of Christ. We must support and encourage one another in living out the truth of the gospel and rejecting legalism.

Cultivating a community of grace involves fostering relationships built on love, trust, and mutual respect. It means creating an environment where people can grow in their faith and experience the freedom of God's grace. By cultivating a community of grace, we can reflect the love and unity of Christ to the world.

Theological Insights from the Allegory

As we delve deeper into the allegory of Hagar and Sarah, several theological insights emerge that are crucial for understanding Paul's message and its implications for our faith.

The nature of God's promise …

The story of Isaac's birth highlights the nature of God's promise: it is miraculous and not dependent on human effort. Isaac's birth was a result of God's intervention and faithfulness, not Abraham and Sarah's ability. This teaches us that God's promises are fulfilled by His power and grace, not by our efforts.

The nature of God's promise underscores the reliability and faithfulness of God. When God makes a promise, He has the power to fulfill it, regardless of human limitations. This understanding deepens our trust in God and assures us that He will accomplish His purposes in our lives.

The role of faith ...

The contrast between Ishmael and Isaac illustrates the centrality of faith in receiving God's promises. Isaac's birth was a result of faith in God's promise, while Ishmael's birth was a result of human effort. This teaches us that faith, not works, is the means by which we receive God's blessings. The role of faith highlights the importance of trusting in God's promises and relying on His grace. Faith is not just intellectual assent but a deep trust in God's character and His ability to fulfill His promises. This trust shapes our relationship with God and our daily lives.

The futility of human effort ...

The story of Ishmael's birth illustrates the futility of relying on human effort to achieve God's purposes. Abraham and Sarah's attempt to fulfill God's promise through Hagar resulted in strife and division. This teaches us that our efforts, apart from God's guidance, are futile and can lead to negative consequences. The futility of human effort underscores the need for reliance on God's grace and guidance. It reminds us that our best efforts are insufficient to achieve God's purposes and that we must depend on His power and wisdom. This reliance leads to a life of humility and dependence on God.

The transformative power of grace

The contrast between the old and new covenants highlights the transformative power of God's grace. The old covenant, based on the law, led to bondage and condemnation. The new covenant, based on grace, leads to freedom and transformation. This teaches us that God's grace has the power to change our lives and set us free from bondage.

The transformative power of grace is at the heart of the gospel message. It is not just about forgiveness of sins but about a new life in Christ, characterized by freedom, joy, and spiritual growth. This transformation is a testimony to the power of God's grace and a witness to the world.

Living Out the Allegory in Our Daily Lives

The allegory of Hagar and Sarah has profound implications for how we live our daily lives as believers.

Living in the freedom of the promise ...

As children of the promise, we are called to live in the freedom that comes from God's grace. This means rejecting legalism and any attempts to earn God's favor through our efforts. Instead, we embrace the freedom and joy that come from being in a right relationship with God through faith in Christ. Living in the freedom of the promise involves a daily commitment to trust in God's grace and to live by faith. It means letting go of the need to control our lives and relying on God's guidance and provision. This freedom leads to a life of peace, joy, and purpose.

Trusting in God's timing ...

The story of Isaac's birth teaches us to trust in God's timing. God fulfilled His promise to Abraham and Sarah in His perfect timing, not according to their schedule. This teaches us to be patient and to trust that God's timing is always best.

Trusting in God's timing involves surrendering our plans and expectations to Him. It means believing that God knows what is best for us and that He will fulfill His promises at the right time. This trust leads to a life of contentment and peace, knowing that God is in control.

Embracing our identity as children of God ...

As children of the promise, we have a new identity in Christ. We are no longer defined by our past or by our efforts to achieve righteousness. Instead, we are defined by God's grace and our relationship with Him. This new identity shapes how we see ourselves and how we live our lives.

Embracing our identity as children of God involves living out this truth in our daily lives. It means seeing ourselves as God sees us and allowing His grace to shape our actions, attitudes, and relationships. This identity empowers us to live in freedom and to reflect Christ's character in all that we do.

Building a community of grace ...

The allegory of Hagar and Sarah teaches us the importance of building a community of grace within the body of Christ. We are called to support and encourage one another in living out the truth of the gospel and rejecting legalism. This community of grace reflects the love and unity of Christ and serves as a witness to the world. Building a community of grace involves fostering relationships built on love, trust, and mutual respect. It means creating an environment where people can grow in their faith and experience the freedom of God's grace. By cultivating a community of grace, we can reflect the love and unity of Christ to the world.

Conclusion

As we conclude our reflection on Galatians 4:21-31, we are reminded of the profound theological truths and practical applications of Paul's allegory of Hagar and Sarah.

Paul's teaching challenges us to embrace our identity as children of promise, to reject legalism and embrace grace, to stand firm in the face of persecution, to celebrate the freedom of the new covenant, and to cultivate a community of grace.

May we be a people who live out these truths with integrity, standing firm in our faith and reflecting the love and grace of Christ in all that we do. Let us strive to maintain the unity of the body of Christ, working together to advance His kingdom and bring glory to His name.

10. STANDING FIRM IN FREEDOM

As we continue our study of Paul's letter to the Galatians, we come to chapter 5. In the first 12 verses, Paul emphasizes the importance of standing firm in the freedom that Christ has won for us and warns against the dangers of returning to the bondage of the law. He calls the Galatians to live by faith and to reject any attempt to be justified by works. This message is crucial for us today as we seek to live out our faith in a world that often values performance over grace. Let us read the passage together:

> **Galatians 5:1-12** *"It is for freedom that Christ has set us free. Stand firm, then, and do not let yourselves be burdened again by a yoke of slavery. Mark my words! I, Paul, tell you that if you let yourselves be circumcised, Christ will be of no value to you at all.*
>
> *Again, I declare to every man who lets himself be circumcised that he is obligated to obey the whole law. You who are trying to be justified by the law have been alienated from Christ; you have fallen away from grace. For through the Spirit, we eagerly await by faith the righteousness for which we hope.*
>
> *For in Christ Jesus neither circumcision nor uncircumcision has any value. The only thing that counts is faith expressing itself through love.*
>
> *You were running a good race. Who cut in on you to keep you from obeying the truth? That kind of persuasion does not come from the one who calls you. "A little yeast works through the whole batch of dough." I am confident in the Lord that you will take no other view. The one who is throwing you into confusion, whoever that may be, will have to pay the penalty.*

Brothers and sisters, if I am still preaching circumcision, why am I still being persecuted? In that case the offense of the cross has been abolished. As for those agitators, I wish they would go the whole way and emasculate themselves!"

The Freedom We Have in Christ (Verse 1)

Paul begins this section with a powerful declaration of the freedom that Christ has won for us.

The purpose of Christ's work …

Paul states, *"It is for freedom that Christ has set us free."* The purpose of Christ's redemptive work is to bring us into a state of true freedom. This freedom is not just a release from the penalty of sin, but a liberation from the power and bondage of sin, the law, and the world's oppressive systems. The freedom which Christ offers us all is holistic, encompassing every aspect of our lives. It is a freedom that allows us to live in the fullness of God's grace and love, unburdened by guilt, fear, or the need to earn God's favour. This freedom is a fundamental aspect of the gospel, highlighting the transformative power of Christ's work on our behalf.

Standing firm in freedom …

Paul exhorts the Galatians, *"Stand firm, then, and do not let yourselves be burdened again by a yoke of slavery."* This command to stand firm implies a conscious and deliberate effort to remain in the freedom that Christ has provided. It involves resisting any attempt to return to the bondage of the law or any other form of legalism. Standing firm in freedom requires vigilance and perseverance. It means recognizing and rejecting any teaching or practice that seeks to undermine the sufficiency of Christ's work.

By standing firm, we affirm our trust in the completed work of Christ and our commitment to living in the liberty He has given us.

The yoke of slavery ...

Paul warns against being burdened again by a yoke of slavery. The imagery of a yoke signifies the heavy and oppressive nature of the law when used as a means of justification. The law, with its numerous regulations and requirements, becomes an unbearable burden for those who seek to be justified by it.

The yoke of slavery represents any system of works-based righteousness that demands human effort to achieve acceptance with God. This yoke stands in stark contrast to the freedom Christ offers, which is based on grace and received through faith. Paul's warning calls us to reject any return to legalism and to embrace the liberating grace of the gospel.

The Consequences of Legalism (Verses 2-4)

Paul outlines the serious consequences of seeking justification through the law.

Christ will be of no value ...

Paul declares, *"Mark my words! I, Paul, tell you that if you let yourselves be circumcised, Christ will be of no value to you at all."* The act of circumcision, in this context, represents a reliance on the law for justification.

Paul warns that if the Galatians choose this path, they nullify the benefits of Christ's work. Choosing to be circumcised as a means of justification indicates a rejection of the sufficiency of Christ's sacrifice.

It implies that Christ's death and resurrection are not enough, and that something more is needed to achieve righteousness. This attitude undermines the core message of the gospel and separates believers from the grace that is in Christ.

Obligated to obey the whole Law ...

Paul continues, *"Again I declare to every man who lets himself be circumcised that he is obligated to obey the whole law."* The law is an indivisible whole, and those who seek to be justified by one part of it are bound to keep all of it. This is an impossible burden, as no one can perfectly keep the entire law. The obligation to obey the whole law highlights the futility and impossibility of achieving righteousness through human effort.

The law's demands are comprehensive and exacting, and failure in even one aspect results in guilt. This reality underscores the need for a different means of justification - one that is based on grace and faith, not works.

Fallen away from grace ...

Paul warns, *"You who are trying to be justified by the law have been alienated from Christ; you have fallen away from grace."* Seeking justification through the law alienates believers from the grace of Christ. It represents a departure from the gospel of grace and a return to a system of works. Falling away from grace does not mean losing salvation but indicates a departure from the principle of grace as the basis for our relationship with God. It involves turning away from the sufficiency of Christ's work and relying on human effort. This departure is a serious error, as it undermines the very foundation of the Christian faith.

Living by Faith (Verses 5-6)

Paul contrasts the futility of legalism with the life of faith empowered by the Spirit.

Eagerly awaiting righteousness ...

Paul states, *"For through the Spirit we eagerly await by faith the righteousness for which we hope."* The life of faith involves a confident expectation of the righteousness that comes through the Spirit. This righteousness is not something we achieve but something we receive by faith.

The righteousness for which we hope is both a present reality and a future expectation. In Christ, we are already declared righteous before God. Yet, we also look forward to the full realization of this righteousness when Christ returns. This eager waiting is characterized by faith and a reliance on the Spirit's work in our lives.

The value of faith expressed through love ...

Paul declares, *"For in Christ Jesus neither circumcision nor uncircumcision has any value. The only thing that counts is faith expressing itself through love."* The external act of circumcision, or the lack thereof, is irrelevant in Christ. What matters is faith that is active and demonstrated through love.

Faith expressing itself through love is the true mark of a believer. Genuine faith results in a transformed life characterized by love for God and others. This love is the fruit of the Spirit and the evidence of a living and active faith. Paul's emphasis on faith and love underscores the essence of the Christian life and the futility of legalistic practices.

The Danger of False Teaching (Verses 7-10)

Paul addresses the influence of false teachers and the need for vigilance.

Who cut in on you? ...

Paul laments, *"You were running a good race. Who cut in on you to keep you from obeying the truth?"* The Galatians were making good progress in their faith, but false teachers had disrupted their course.

Paul's question highlights the disruptive and harmful influence of these teachers. The imagery of running a race emphasizes the importance of perseverance and focus in the Christian life. False teaching is like an obstacle that hinders our progress and diverts us from the truth.

Paul's lament calls us to be vigilant and discerning, ensuring that we remain on the path of truth and avoid being led astray.

That kind of persuasion ...

Paul states, *"That kind of persuasion does not come from the one who calls you."* The false teachers' influence is not from God, who calls believers to freedom and truth. Their persuasion leads away from the gospel and into bondage. Understanding the source of persuasion is crucial for discernment. God's call leads to freedom, truth, and life.

Any teaching that leads to bondage, error, or confusion is not from God. By discerning the source of teaching, we can protect ourselves from deception and remain anchored in the truth of the gospel.

A little yeast…

Paul warns, *"A little yeast works through the whole batch of dough."* False teaching, like yeast, can spread and permeate the entire community, leading to widespread error and confusion. Even a small amount of false teaching can have significant and harmful effects.

The analogy of yeast emphasizes the insidious nature of false teaching. It can start quite small but quickly spread, affecting the entire community. This warning calls us to be vigilant in guarding the purity of the gospel and to address false teaching promptly and decisively.

Confidence in the Lord …

Paul expresses his confidence, *"I am confident in the Lord that you will take no other view. The one who is throwing you into confusion, whoever that may be, will have to pay the penalty."* Despite the current confusion, Paul is confident that the Galatians will return to the truth. He also warns that those who are causing confusion will face consequences.

Paul's confidence is rooted in the Lord, not in the Galatians' ability. He trusts that God will bring them back to the truth. This confidence encourages us to trust in God's faithfulness and to be patient and hopeful in the face of challenges. It also serves as a warning to those who lead others astray, reminding them of the serious consequences of their actions.

The Offense of the Cross (Verses 11-12)

Paul addresses the issue of persecution and the offense of the cross.

Persecution for the cross ...

Paul asks, *"Brothers and sisters, if I am still preaching circumcision, why am I still being persecuted? In that case the offense of the cross has been abolished."* Paul's persecution is evidence that he is preaching the true gospel, which centers on the cross of Christ. If he were preaching circumcision, he would not face opposition. The cross is inherently offensive because it challenges human pride and self-sufficiency. It declares that salvation is not achieved by human effort but received as a gift through faith in Christ's finished work. This message is countercultural and often met with resistance. Paul's persecution underscores the radical nature of the gospel and the opposition it can provoke.

The offense of the cross ...

The offense of the cross lies in its message of grace and dependence on Christ alone for salvation. It confronts the human desire to earn and achieve righteousness through personal effort. The cross declares that human efforts are insufficient and that only through Christ's sacrifice can we be reconciled to God. Understanding the offense of the cross helps us appreciate the radical nature of the gospel. It calls us to humility and dependence on God's grace, rejecting any reliance on our efforts. This message is liberating, as it frees us from the burden of trying to earn God's favor and invites us to rest in His grace.

Paul's strong language ...

Paul concludes with strong language: *"As for those agitators, I wish they would go the whole way and emasculate themselves!"* This harsh statement reflects Paul's intense frustration with the false teachers and their harmful influence.

It emphasizes the seriousness of their error and the need for decisive action. Paul's strong language serves as a stark warning about the dangers of false teaching. It underscores the importance of protecting the purity of the gospel and the well-being of the community. By addressing false teaching decisively, we can prevent its spread and maintain the integrity of the gospel.

Practical Applications for Our Lives

How then shall we live in light of Galatians 5:1-12?

Stand firm in the freedom of Christ ...

Paul's exhortation to stand firm in the freedom Christ has won for us challenges us to embrace and live out this freedom daily. We must resist any attempt to return to legalism or works-based righteousness and instead trust in the sufficiency of Christ's work. Standing firm in freedom involves a conscious and deliberate effort to remain grounded in the gospel of grace. It means rejecting any teaching or practice that seeks to undermine the sufficiency of Christ's work and embracing the liberty that comes from living in the truth of the gospel.

Reject legalism and embrace grace ...

Paul's warning about the consequences of legalism calls us to reject any system that seeks to justify us by our efforts. We must embrace the grace that comes through faith in Christ and live in the freedom and joy it brings.

Rejecting legalism involves a commitment to living by faith and relying on God's grace. It means letting go of the need to earn God's favor and trusting in the sufficiency of Christ's work. By embracing grace, we can experience the freedom and joy that come from being in a right relationship with God.

Live by faith, expressed through love …

Paul's emphasis on faith expressing itself through love challenges us to live out our faith in practical ways. Genuine faith results in a transformed life characterized by love for God and others. Living by faith expressed through love involves a daily commitment to love God and to love others. It means allowing the Holy Spirit to work in us and through us, producing the fruit of love in our lives. This love is the evidence of a living and active faith and reflects the character of Christ to the world.

Be vigilant against false teaching…

Paul's warning about the influence of false teachers calls us to be vigilant and discerning. We must guard the purity of the gospel and be aware of any teaching or practice that seeks to lead us astray. Being vigilant against false teaching involves a commitment to knowing and understanding the truth of the gospel. It means being discerning in our choice of leaders and influencers and being willing to address false teaching promptly and decisively. By guarding the purity of the gospel, we can protect ourselves and our community from deception.

Embrace the offense of the cross …

Paul's discussion of the offense of the cross challenges us to embrace the radical nature of the gospel. We must be willing to face opposition and persecution for the sake of the truth and to rely on God's grace for our salvation. Embracing the offense of the cross involves a commitment to humility and dependence on God's grace. It means rejecting any reliance on our efforts and trusting in the sufficiency of Christ's work.

By embracing the offense of the cross, we can experience the freedom and joy that come from being in a right relationship with God.

Theological Insights from the Passage

As we delve deeper into Galatians 5:1-12, several important theological insights emerge which we must embrace in our understanding of Paul's message and its implications for our faith.

The sufficiency of Christ's work ...

Paul's warning here about the consequences of seeking justification through the law underscores the sufficiency of Christ's work. Christ's death and resurrection are sufficient for our salvation, and any attempt to add to it undermines the gospel.

The sufficiency of the work of Jesus Christ highlights the completeness and finality of His sacrifice. It assures us that there is nothing more we need to do to be accepted by God. This understanding deepens our trust in Christ and frees us from the burden of trying to earn God's favour.

The role of the Holy Spirit ...

Paul's emphasis on living by the Spirit and awaiting righteousness by faith highlights the role of the Holy Spirit in the believer's life. The Spirit empowers us to live in the freedom of the gospel and to produce the fruit of love. The role of the Holy Spirit is central to the Christian life. The Spirit indwells believers, guiding, empowering, and transforming them. By relying on the Holy Spirit, we can live in the freedom and fullness of the gospel and reflect the character of Christ in our lives.

The nature of justification ...

Paul's discussion of justification by faith versus justification by the law clearly underscores the nature of justification. Justification is a gift received by faith, not a reward earned by works.

The nature of justification highlights the grace and mercy of God. It assures us that our standing before God is not based on our performance but on His grace. This understanding frees us from the burden of trying to earn God's favor and invites us to rest in His grace.

The danger of legalism ...

Paul's warning about the consequences of legalism highlights the danger of relying on human effort for justification. Legalism leads to bondage and alienation from Christ. The danger of legalism underscores the importance of relying on God's grace for our salvation. It reminds us that our efforts are insufficient to achieve righteousness and that we must trust in the sufficiency of Christ's work. By rejecting legalism, we can experience the freedom and joy that come from living in the truth of the gospel.

The transformative power of grace ...

Paul's emphasis on faith expressing itself through love highlights the transformative power of God's grace. Grace not only justifies us but also transforms us, producing the fruit of love in our lives. The transformative power of grace is at the heart of the gospel message. It is not just about forgiveness of sins but about a new life in Christ, characterized by freedom, joy, and spiritual growth. This transformation is a testimony to the power of God's grace and a witness to the world.

Living Out the Truth of the Passage

The teachings of Galatians 5:1-12 have quite profound implications for how we live our daily lives as believers.

Embrace the freedom of the Gospel ...

Paul's exhortation to stand firm in the freedom Christ has won for us challenges us to embrace and live out this freedom daily. We must resist any attempt to return to legalism or works-based righteousness and instead trust in the sufficiency of Christ's work.

Embracing the freedom of the gospel involves a daily commitment to trust in God's grace and to live by faith. It means letting go of the need to control our lives and relying on God's guidance and provision. This freedom leads to a life of peace, joy, and purpose.

Trust in the sufficiency of Christ's work ...

The Apostle Paul's warning about the consequences of seeking justification through the law calls us to trust in the sufficiency of Christ's work. We must rely on His sacrifice for our salvation and reject any attempt to add to it. Trusting in the sufficiency of Christ's work involves a deep reliance on His grace and a rejection of any reliance on our efforts. It means believing that His work is complete and that we are fully accepted by God because of Him. This trust leads to a life of rest and assurance in God's love.

Live by the Spirit ...

Paul's emphasis on living by the Spirit challenges us to rely on the Holy Spirit for guidance and empowerment. The Spirit empowers us to live in the freedom of the gospel and to produce the fruit of love.

Living by the Spirit involves a daily commitment to seek the Spirit's guidance and to rely on His power. It means allowing the Spirit to work in us and through us, producing the fruit of love in our lives. By living by the Spirit, we can experience the fullness of the gospel and reflect the character of Christ in our lives.

Cultivate a community of grace ...

Paul's teaching encourages us to cultivate a community of grace within the body of Christ. We must support and encourage one another in living out the truth of the gospel and rejecting legalism. Cultivating a community of grace involves fostering relationships built on love, trust, and mutual respect. It means creating an environment where people can grow in their faith and experience the freedom of God's grace. By cultivating a community of grace, we can reflect the love and unity of Christ to the world.

Conclusion

As we conclude our reflection on Galatians 5:1-12, we are reminded of the profound theological truths and practical applications of Paul's message. Paul's teaching challenges us to embrace our identity as children of promise, to reject legalism and embrace grace, to stand firm in the face of persecution, to celebrate the freedom of the new covenant, and to cultivate a community of grace.

May we be a people who live out these truths with integrity, standing firm in our faith and reflecting the love and grace of Christ in all that we do. Let us strive to maintain the unity of the body of Christ, working together to advance His kingdom and bring glory to His name.

11. WALKING IN THE SPIRIT

In the second half of Galatians 5, we find Paul explaining what it means to live out the freedom we have in Christ by walking in the Spirit. He contrasts the works of the flesh with the fruit of the Spirit and provides practical guidance for living a life that reflects the character of Christ. This message is crucial for us today as we seek to live out our faith in a world that often pulls us in conflicting directions. Let us read the passage together:

> **Galatians 5:13-26** *"You, my brothers and sisters, were called to be free. But do not use your freedom to indulge the flesh; rather, serve one another humbly in love. For the entire law is fulfilled in keeping this one command: 'Love your neighbor as yourself.'" If you bite and devour each other, watch out or you will be destroyed by each other.*
>
> *So, I say, walk by the Spirit, and you will not gratify the desires of the flesh. For the flesh desires what is contrary to the Spirit, and the Spirit what is contrary to the flesh. They are in conflict with each other, so that you are not to do whatever you want. But if you are led by the Spirit, you are not under the law.*
>
> *The acts of the flesh are obvious: sexual immorality, impurity and debauchery; idolatry and witchcraft; hatred, discord, jealousy, fits of rage, selfish ambition, dissensions, factions and envy; drunkenness, orgies, and the like. I warn you, as I did before, that those who live like this will not inherit the kingdom of God.*
>
> *But the fruit of the Spirit is love, joy, peace, forbearance, kindness, goodness, faithfulness, gentleness and self-control. Against such things there is no law.*

Those who belong to Christ Jesus have crucified the flesh with its passions and desires. Since we live by the Spirit, let us keep in step with the Spirit. Let us not become conceited, provoking and envying each other."

The Call to Freedom (Verses 13-15)

Paul begins this section by emphasizing the purpose of our calling to freedom in Christ.

Called to be free ...

Paul states, *"You, my brothers and sisters, were called to be free."* This declaration highlights the essence of the Christian life: freedom. This freedom is a fundamental aspect of the gospel, given to us through Christ's redemptive work. It is a freedom from the law, sin, and death, allowing us to live in the fullness of God's grace and love.

The call to freedom is a call to live as God intended, unburdened by the demands and condemnation of the law. It is a call to experience the abundant life that Jesus promised, characterized by joy, peace, and righteousness. This freedom is an end in itself, but also a means to live out God's purposes in our lives.

Freedom misused ...

Paul warns, *"But do not use your freedom to indulge the flesh; rather, serve one another humbly in love."* Freedom in Christ is not a license to sin or to live selfishly. It is an opportunity to serve others and to live out the love that Christ has shown us. Using freedom to indulge the flesh leads to self-centeredness and destructive behaviour. It undermines the purpose of our freedom and damages our relationships with others.

Fulfillment of the Law ...

Paul continues, *"For the entire law is fulfilled in keeping this one command: 'Love your neighbor as yourself.'"* Love is the fulfillment of the law.

When we love others as ourselves, we naturally fulfill the requirements of the law, because love always seeks the well-being of others and avoids harm.

The command to love our neighbour as ourselves is central to the Christian ethic. It encapsulates the essence of the law and the teachings of Jesus.

By focusing on love, we fulfill the law's demands and live in a way that reflects the character of Christ. This love is not a mere feeling but a deliberate action that seeks the good of others.

Warning against destructive behaviour ...

Paul warns, *"If you bite and devour each other, watch out or you will be destroyed by each other."* Conflict, division, and destructive behaviour are contrary to the freedom we have in Christ.

They harm the community and hinder our witness to the world. The warning against biting and devouring each other underscores the importance of unity and love within the body of Christ.

Destructive behaviour always harms individuals and also damages the community as a whole. By avoiding such behaviour and cultivating love and unity, we can build a strong and healthy community that reflects the love of Christ.

Walking by the Spirit (Verses 16-18)

Paul transitions to the practical implications of living out our freedom by walking in the Spirit.

Walking by the Spirit ...

Paul exhorts, *"So I say, walk by the Spirit, and you will not gratify the desires of the flesh."* Walking by the Spirit is the key to living out our freedom in Christ. It involves living in step with the Holy Spirit, allowing Him to guide and empower us in our daily lives. Walking by the Spirit is a dynamic and ongoing process. It requires attentiveness to the Spirit's leading and a willingness to follow His guidance. By walking by the Spirit, we can overcome the desires of the flesh and live in a way that pleases God.

Conflictb flesh and Spirit ...

Paul explains, *"For the flesh desires what is contrary to the Spirit, and the Spirit what is contrary to the flesh. They are in conflict with each other, so that you are not to do whatever you want."* The flesh and the Spirit are in opposition to each other, creating a conflict within us.

This conflict is a normal part of the Christian experience. The flesh represents our old, sinful nature, while the Spirit represents our new, redeemed nature in Christ. This internal struggle highlights the need for reliance on the Spirit's power to overcome the desires of the flesh.

Led by the Spirit ...

Paul reassures, *"But if you are led by the Spirit, you are not under the law."* Being led by the Spirit frees us from the constraints and condemnation of the law.

The Spirit empowers us to live in a way that fulfills the law's requirements through love and grace. Being led by the Spirit involves a daily surrender to His guidance and an openness to His work in our lives. It means trusting that the Spirit will lead us in the right direction and enable us to live according to God's will. This reliance on the Spirit frees us from the burden of trying to achieve righteousness through our efforts.

The Works of the Flesh (Verses 19-21)

Paul provides a detailed list of the works of the flesh, contrasting them with the fruit of the Spirit.

Obvious acts of the flesh ...

Paul states, *"The acts of the flesh are obvious: sexual immorality, impurity and debauchery; idolatry and witchcraft; hatred, discord, jealousy, fits of rage, selfish ambition, dissensions, factions and envy; drunkenness, orgies, and the like."* These acts are manifestations of our sinful nature and are contrary to the Spirit's work. The list of the acts of the flesh is comprehensive and includes both obvious and subtle sins. It highlights the destructive nature of the flesh and its tendency to lead us away from God's will. These acts damage our relationship with God and others and hinder our spiritual growth.

Consequences of living by the flesh ...

Paul warns, *"I warn you, as I did before, that those who live like this will not inherit the kingdom of God."* Living according to the flesh has serious consequences, including exclusion from the kingdom of God. This warning underscores the importance of living by the Spirit and rejecting the desires of the flesh.

The warning against living by the flesh emphasizes the incompatibility of such a lifestyle with the values of God's kingdom. It calls us to examine our lives and to turn away from behaviors that are contrary to God's will. By living by the Spirit, we can inherit the kingdom of God and experience the fullness of life that He offers.

The Fruit of the Spirit (Verses 22-23)

Paul contrasts the works of the flesh with the fruit of the Spirit, highlighting the characteristics of a life led by the Spirit.

Characteristics of the fruit of the Spirit ...

Paul declares, *"But the fruit of the Spirit is love, joy, peace, forbearance, kindness, goodness, faithfulness, gentleness and self-control. Against such things there is no law."*

The fruit of the Spirit represents the qualities that the Spirit produces in the life of a believer. The list of the fruit of the Spirit includes both inward and outward qualities. These qualities reflect the character of Christ and are the evidence of the Spirit's work in our lives. They stand in stark contrast to the works of the flesh and demonstrate the transformative power of the Spirit.

No law against the fruit of the Spirit ...

Paul emphasizes, *"Against such things there is no law."* The qualities produced by the Spirit are in harmony with God's will and are not subject to the condemnation of the law. They fulfill the law's requirements through love and grace. The absence of a law against the fruit of the Spirit highlights the positive and affirming nature of these qualities.

They are the natural outworking of a life led by the Spirit and are pleasing to God. By cultivating the fruit of the Spirit, we can live in a way that honors God and blesses others.

Crucifying the Flesh (Verses 24-25)

Paul explains the process of overcoming the flesh by crucifying it and living by the Spirit.

Crucified with Christ ...

Paul states, *"Those who belong to Christ Jesus have crucified the flesh with its passions and desires."* Belonging to Christ involves a decisive break with our old, sinful nature. By faith, we have crucified the flesh and its desires, identifying with Christ's life, death and resurrection.

Crucifying the flesh is an ongoing process that requires daily commitment and surrender. It involves rejecting the desires of the flesh and choosing to live by the Spirit. This process is empowered by the Spirit and is a vital aspect of our sanctification.

Living by the Spirit ...

Paul exhorts, *"Since we live by the Spirit, let us keep in step with the Spirit."* Living by the Spirit involves a continuous and dynamic relationship with the Holy Spirit. It requires attentiveness to His guidance and a willingness to follow His lead. Keeping in step with the Spirit means aligning our lives with His direction and allowing Him to shape our thoughts, our attitudes, and our actions. It involves a daily surrender to His work and a commitment to live according to His will. By keeping in step with the Spirit, we can experience the fullness of life that He offers.

Avoiding Conceit and Provocation (Verse 26)

Paul concludes with a warning against attitudes and behaviors that undermine the unity and love within the body of Christ.

Avoiding conceit...

Paul warns, *"Let us not become conceited."* Conceit is an attitude of self-importance and superiority that undermines relationships and community. It leads to pride and division, hindering the work of the Spirit in our lives.

Avoiding conceit involves cultivating humility and recognizing our dependence on God's grace. It means valuing others and their contributions and avoiding attitudes of superiority. By embracing humility, we can build a strong and healthy community that reflects the love of Christ.

Avoiding provocation and envy ...

Paul then continues, *"provoking and envying each other."* Provocation and envy are destructive behaviors that damage relationships and hinder the unity of the body of Christ. They create conflict and division, undermining the work of the Spirit.

Avoiding provocation and envy involves cultivating love and respect for others. It means celebrating their successes and supporting them in their struggles.

By embracing love and unity, we can build a community that reflects the character of Christ and the fruit of the Spirit.

Practical Applications for Our Lives

As we reflect on Galatians 5:13-26, several practical applications emerge for our lives today.

Embrace the call to freedom ...

Paul's teaching challenges us to embrace the freedom we have in Christ. This freedom is not a license to sin but an opportunity to serve others and to live out the love of Christ. We must use our freedom to build up others and to reflect the character of Christ in our lives.

Embracing the call to freedom involves a daily commitment to live according to God's will and to serve others in love. It means rejecting self-centeredness and embracing the selfless love that Christ has shown us. By living in this freedom, we can experience the fullness of life that God intends for us.

Walk by the Spirit ...

Paul's exhortation to walk by the Spirit challenges us to rely on the Holy Spirit for guidance and empowerment. We must cultivate a dynamic and ongoing relationship with the Spirit, allowing Him to lead and shape our lives. Walking by the Spirit involves a daily surrender to His guidance and a willingness to follow His lead. It means being attentive to His promptings and open to His work in our lives. By walking by the Spirit, we can overcome the desires of the flesh and glorify God.

Cultivate the fruit of the Spirit ...

Paul's description of the fruit of the Spirit challenges us to cultivate these qualities in our lives.

We must allow the Holy Spirit to work in us and through us, producing love, joy, peace, forbearance, kindness, goodness, faithfulness, gentleness, and self-control. Cultivating the fruit of the Spirit involves a daily commitment to live according to God's will and to reflect His character. It means allowing the Spirit to transform our thoughts, attitudes, and actions. By cultivating the fruit of the Spirit, we can live in a way that honors God and blesses others.

Crucify the flesh ...

Paul's teaching on crucifying the flesh challenges us to reject the desires of our old, sinful nature. We must identify with Christ's death and resurrection, allowing Him to transform us and to empower us to live according to His will. Crucifying the flesh involves a daily commitment to reject sin and to live according to God's will. It means recognizing the destructive nature of the flesh and choosing to live by the Spirit. By crucifying the flesh, we can experience the freedom and transformation that come from living in Christ.

Conclusion

In Galatians 5:13-26, Paul reminds the Galatian believers, and us, that we are called to be free in Christ, but this freedom should not be used to indulge in sinful desires. Instead, we are to serve one another in love, fulfilling the law through the command to "love your neighbor as yourself."

Paul warns against behaviors driven by selfishness, which can lead to destructive conflicts, and urges them to "walk by the Spirit" to avoid gratifying the desires of the flesh.

He lists the "acts of the flesh" and warns that those who live in this way will not inherit the kingdom of God.

In contrast, Paul describes the "fruit of the Spirit" as qualities like love, joy, peace, patience, kindness, goodness, faithfulness, gentleness, and self-control. He emphasizes that there is no law against these virtues. Those who belong to Christ have crucified the flesh with its passions and desires and are called to live by the Spirit. Paul concludes by encouraging believers to stay in step with the Spirit, cultivating the virtues that reflect their new life in Christ.

This letter may have been addressed to believers on the other side of the world 2,000 years ago, but the Holy Spirit has preserved this text for us today and I really encourage you to reflect on these verses some more in the coming days as the Spirit reminds us of the incredible freedom which is ours in Christ.

12. LIVING IN CHRIST

We now conclude our journey through Paul's letter to the Galatians, as we focus on chapter six. In this final chapter, Paul provides practical instructions for living out the Christian faith within the community of believers. He emphasizes the importance of bearing one another's burdens, sowing to the Spirit, and boasting in the cross of Christ. This passage is rich with insights that can guide us in our daily walk with the Lord and in our relationships with one another.

> **Galatians 6:1-18** *"Brothers and sisters, if someone is caught in a sin, you who live by the Spirit should restore that person gently. But watch yourselves, or you also may be tempted. Carry each other's burdens, and in this way, you will fulfill the law of Christ. If anyone thinks they are something when they are not, they deceive themselves. Each one should test their own actions. Then they can take pride in themselves alone, without comparing themselves to someone else, for each one should carry their own load. Nevertheless, the one who receives instruction in the word should share all good things with their instructor.*
>
> *Do not be deceived: God cannot be mocked. A man reaps what he sows. Whoever sows to please their flesh, from the flesh will reap destruction; whoever sows to please the Spirit, from the Spirit will reap eternal life. Let us not become weary in doing good, for at the proper time we will reap a harvest if we do not give up. Therefore, as we have opportunity, let us do good to all people, especially to those who belong to the family of believers.*
>
> *See what large letters I use as I write to you with my own hand! Those who want to impress people by means of the flesh are trying to compel you to be circumcised.*

The only reason they do this is to avoid being persecuted for the cross of Christ. Not even those who are circumcised keep the law, yet they want you to be circumcised that they may boast about your circumcision in the flesh. May I never boast except in the cross of our Lord Jesus Christ, through which the world has been crucified to me, and I to the world.

Neither circumcision nor uncircumcision means anything; what counts is the new creation. Peace and mercy to all who follow this rule - to the Israel of God. From now on, let no one cause me trouble, for I bear on my body the marks of Jesus. The grace of our Lord Jesus Christ be with your spirit, brothers and sisters. Amen."

Bearing One Another's Burdens (Verses 1-5)

Paul begins this chapter with a call to mutual accountability and support within the community of believers.

Restoring with gentleness ...

Paul instructs, "*Brothers and sisters, if someone is caught in a sin, you who live by the Spirit should restore that person gently. But watch yourselves, or you also may be tempted.*" Restoration is a crucial aspect of Christian community. When someone falls into sin, those who are spiritually mature should seek to restore them with gentleness and humility.

The emphasis on gentleness reflects the compassionate nature of Christ. Restoration should be done with a spirit of love and understanding, not harshness or judgment. The goal is to bring the person back into a right relationship with God and the community. This process requires sensitivity to the individual's struggles and a commitment to their spiritual well-being.

Carrying each other's burdens ...

Paul continues, *"Carry each other's burdens, and in this way you will fulfill the law of Christ."* Bearing one another's burdens is a practical expression of love and compassion. It involves helping others with their struggles, whether they are spiritual, emotional, or physical. The law of Christ, as Paul refers to it, is the law of love. Jesus taught that the greatest commandments are to love God and to love our neighbors as ourselves (Matthew 22:37-39).

By carrying each other's burdens, we will always fulfill this commandment and reflect the love of Jesus Christ in our relationships. This mutual support helps to strengthen the community and enables us to grow together in faith.

Avoiding self-deception ...

Paul warns, *"If anyone thinks they are something when they are not, they deceive themselves."* Pride and self-deception can hinder our ability to help others and to grow spiritually. We must have an accurate understanding of ourselves and our limitations. Avoiding self-deception involves humility and self-awareness. We must recognize our own need for God's grace and avoid comparing ourselves to others. By focusing on our relationship with God and our own spiritual growth, we can avoid the pitfalls of pride and self-righteousness.

Personal responsibility ...

Paul instructs, *"Each one should test their own actions. Then they can take pride in themselves alone, without comparing themselves to someone else, for each one should carry their own load."* While we are called to bear one another's burdens, we also have personal responsibilities that we must carry.

Testing our own actions involves self-examination and accountability. We must evaluate our motives and actions in light of God's word and seek to live in accordance with His will. Personal responsibility does not negate mutual support but complements it, as each member of the community contributes to the overall health and growth of the body of Christ.

Sowing and Reaping (Verses 6-10)

Paul introduces the principle of sowing and reaping, emphasizing the importance of living according to the Spirit.

Sharing with instructors ...

Paul states, *"Nevertheless, the one who receives instruction in the word should share all good things with their instructor."* This principle highlights the importance of supporting those who teach and lead in the church. Sharing with instructors includes providing for their material needs and encouraging them in their ministry. Supporting those who teach the word of God is a practical expression of gratitude and respect. It recognizes the value of their work and ensures that they can continue to serve effectively. This support strengthens the church and enables it to fulfill its mission.

The principle of sowing and reaping ...

Paul warns, *"Do not be deceived: God cannot be mocked. A man reaps what he sows. Whoever sows to please their flesh, from the flesh will reap destruction; whoever sows to please the Spirit, from the Spirit will reap eternal life."* This principle underscores the importance of our actions and their consequences.

Sowing to please the flesh involves living according to our sinful nature, pursuing selfish desires and temporary pleasures. This leads to destruction and separation from God. In contrast, sowing to please the Spirit involves living according to God's will, pursuing righteousness and spiritual growth. This leads to eternal life and a deeper relationship with God.

Perseverance in doing good ...

Paul encourages, "Let us not become weary in doing good, for at the proper time we will reap a harvest if we do not give up." Perseverance in doing good is essential, even when it is challenging or discouraging. The promise of a future harvest motivates us to continue living according to God's will.

Perseverance involves maintaining our commitment to God's work and trusting in His timing. It requires faith and patience, knowing that our efforts will bear fruit in due season. By persevering in doing good, we can make a lasting impact for God's kingdom and experience His blessings.

Doing good to all ...

Paul concludes, "Therefore, as we have opportunity, let us do good to all people, especially to those who belong to the family of believers." Our responsibility to do good extends to all people, but we have a special obligation to care for our fellow believers. Doing good to all involves a proactive approach to serving others and meeting their needs. It reflects the love of Christ and builds bridges within and outside the church. By prioritizing the family of believers, we strengthen the church and demonstrate the unity and love that should characterize the body of Christ.

Boasting in the Cross (Verses 11-18)

Paul concludes his letter with a personal appeal and a focus on the centrality of the cross of Christ.

Personal appeal ...

Paul writes, *"See what large letters I use as I write to you with my own hand!"* This personal touch emphasizes the importance of Paul's message and his deep concern for the Galatians. Writing in large letters may indicate his urgency and passion or a physical limitation, such as poor eyesight. Paul's personal appeal underscores his genuine care and commitment to the Galatians. It reflects his pastoral heart and his desire for them to understand and embrace the truth of the gospel. This personal touch adds weight to his message and connects with the readers on a deeper level.

The motives of false teachers ...

Paul exposes the motives of the false teachers: *"Those who want to impress people by means of the flesh are trying to compel you to be circumcised. The only reason they do this is to avoid being persecuted for the cross of Christ. Not even those who are circumcised keep the law, yet they want you to be circumcised that they may boast about your circumcision in the flesh."*

The false teachers were motivated by a desire to impress others and avoid persecution. The false teachers sought to Impose circumcision as a means of gaining approval and avoiding persecution. Their focus on external conformity rather than genuine faith revealed their misguided priorities. Paul's critique highlights the danger of seeking human approval over God's approval and the futility of external rituals without a transformed heart.

Boasting in the cross ...

Paul declares, *"May I never boast except in the cross of our Lord Jesus Christ, through which the world has been crucified to me, and I to the world."* Paul's only boast is in the cross of Christ, the symbol of God's ultimate sacrifice and redemption.

Boasting in the cross means recognizing that our salvation and identity are rooted in Christ's work on the cross. It involves a rejection of worldly values and a commitment to living for God's glory. The cross is the foundation of our faith and the source of our hope, and it should be the focus of our lives and our message.

The new creation ...

Paul emphasizes, *"Neither circumcision nor uncircumcision means anything; what counts is the new creation."* The new creation is the result of Christ's redemptive work, transforming us from the inside out. The new creation is characterized by a transformed heart and life, reflecting the character of Christ. It involves a break from our old, sinful nature and a commitment to living according to God's will. This transformation is the true mark of a believer, not external rituals or practices.

Peace and mercy ...

Paul concludes, *"Peace and mercy to all who follow this rule - to the Israel of God."* Those who live according to the new creation experience God's peace and mercy. The Israel of God refers to the community of believers who are united in Christ. Peace and mercy are the blessings of living in accordance with God's will and experiencing His grace. They are the fruit of a life transformed by the gospel and lived in the power of the Spirit.

By embracing the new creation, we can experience the fullness of God's blessings and reflect His character to the world.

Paul's final words...

Paul writes, *"From now on, let no one cause me trouble, for I bear on my body the marks of Jesus. The grace of our Lord Jesus Christ be with your spirit, brothers and sisters. Amen."* Paul's final words reflect his deep commitment to Christ and his desire for the Galatians to experience God's grace. Paul's reference to the marks of Jesus may refer to the physical scars and suffering he endured for the sake of the gospel. These marks are a testament to his faithfulness and commitment to Christ. His final blessing emphasizes the centrality of God's grace in the Christian life and his deep love for the Galatian believers.

Practical Applications for Our Lives

As we reflect on these final words, several practical applications emerge for our lives today.

Restore with gentleness ...

Paul's instruction to restore those caught in sin with gentleness challenges us to always approach others with compassion and humility. We must always seek to restore relationships and individuals with a spirit of love and understanding. Restoring others with gentleness involves recognizing our own need for grace and approaching others with humility. It means being patient and compassionate, seeking to bring healing and reconciliation. By restoring with gentleness, we reflect the character of Christ and build a stronger, more supportive community.

Bear one another's burdens ...

Paul's call to bear one another's burdens, challenging s to support and care for each other in practical ways. We must be willing to share in the struggles and challenges of others, offering help and encouragement. Bearing one another's burdens involves a commitment to being present and supportive in the lives of others. It means offering practical help, emotional support, and spiritual encouragement. By bearing one another's burdens, we fulfill the law of Christ and build a community characterized by love and compassion.

Test our own actions...

Paul's instruction to test our own actions challenges us to engage in regular self-examination and accountability. We must evaluate our motives and actions in light of God's word and seek to live according to His will.

Testing our own actions involves being honest with ourselves and seeking God's guidance in our lives. It means avoiding comparisons with others and focusing on our own spiritual growth. By testing our own actions, we can live with integrity and authenticity, reflecting the character of Christ.

Sow to please the Spirit ...

Paul's teaching on sowing and reaping challenges us to live according to the Spirit, pursuing righteousness and spiritual growth. We must invest our time and resources in things that honor God and build His kingdom. Sowing to please the Spirit involves making intentional choices that align with God's will. It means prioritizing spiritual growth, serving others, and living in obedience to God.

By sowing to please the Spirit, we can reap the rewards of a life lived for God and experience His blessings.

Persevere in doing good ...

Paul's encouragement to persevere in doing good challenges us to remain steadfast in our commitment to God's work, even when it is difficult. We must trust in God's timing and continue to serve faithfully. Persevering in doing good involves maintaining our focus on God's purposes and trusting that our efforts will bear fruit. It means being patient and persistent, even when we face challenges or discouragement. By persevering in doing good, we can make a lasting impact for God's kingdom and experience His faithfulness.

Support those who teach ...

Paul's instruction to share with those who teach challenges us to support and encourage our leaders and instructors. We must recognize the value of their work and provide for their needs. Supporting those who teach involves offering practical help, financial support, and encouragement. It means recognizing the importance of their ministry and ensuring that they can serve effectively. By supporting those who teach, we strengthen the church and enable it to fulfill its mission.

Boast in the cross ...

Paul's focus on boasting in the cross challenges us to center our lives on Christ's work and to reject worldly values. We must find our identity and purpose in the cross and live for God's glory. Boasting in the cross involves recognizing that our salvation and identity are rooted in Christ's work.

It means rejecting the values and priorities of the world and living for God's glory. By boasting in the cross, we can experience the fullness of life that comes from living for Christ and reflecting His character.

Embrace the new creation ...

Paul's emphasis on the new creation challenges us to live out our transformed identity in Christ. We must reject our old, sinful nature and embrace the new life that God has given us. Embracing the new creation involves living according to God's will and allowing Him to transform us from the inside out. It means reflecting the character of Christ in our thoughts, attitudes, and actions.

By embracing the new creation, we can experience the fullness of God's blessings and make a lasting impact for His kingdom.

Conclusion

As we conclude our reflection on Galatians 6:1-18, we are reminded of the profound theological truths and practical applications of Paul's message. Paul's teaching challenges us to restore with gentleness, bear one another's burdens, test our own actions, sow to please the Spirit, persevere in doing good, support those who teach, boast in the cross, and embrace the new creation.

May we be a people who live out these truths with integrity, standing firm in our faith and reflecting the love and grace of Christ in all that we do. Let us strive to maintain the unity of the body of Christ, working together to advance His kingdom and bring glory to His name.

www.ingramcontent.com/pod-product-compliance
Lightning Source LLC
Chambersburg PA
CBHW052221090526
44585CB00015BA/1263